S0-AVD-988

CALIFORNIA MINING TOWN
NEWSPAPERS, 1850-1880

400 Copies
of which 350 copies are for sale

California Mining Town Newspapers, 1850-1880

A Bibliography Compiled by

HELEN S. GIFFEN

San Fernando Valley, California . . . 1954

J. E. REYNOLDS, BOOKSELLER . . . VAN NUYS

COMPOSED AND PRINTED AT THE WESTERNLORE PRESS

Library of Congress Catalog Number 54-9892

PRINTED IN THE UNITED STATES OF AMERICA
WESTERNLORE PRESS

A Note On The Author

BORN in Alabama, Helen S. Giffen became a "native" Californian at the age of one year, when her parents moved to the Los Angeles area. Her interest in the history of early California began when, as a small girl, she explored the Mission San Gabriel, even falling into the old wall of cactus surrounding the mission orchard, thereby receiving a baptism of thorns.

Her youthful curiosity developed into the mature interest of the historian, tempered with a knowledge that many historians lack: that the things of the past impose influences on the present far beyond our conscious recognition. Her study of California and Southwest history was intensified by association with the Southwest Museum, where she was first librarian of the Munk Library of Arizoniana. This period of librarianship was to have a lasting influence, and has kept her in the field of historical research.

After her marriage Mrs. Giffen, in company with her husband, undertook a survey of the extant adobe houses of early California. Some fifteen years were spent photographing them in black and white and kodachrome. The result was a pictorial history of approximately 1800 photographs of these adobes, from the Mexican border to the Oregon line.

Interest in the adobe houses of early California did not prevent her from doing field work and research in many phases of western history. *Westways*, the *Southern California Historical Society Quarterly*, and other publications devoted to the west record her work. One of the first full-length biographies of General Mariano Guadalupe Vallejo was written by Mrs. Giffen and appeared serially in the *Pony Express Courier*. With Arthur Woodward, Mrs. Giffen co-authored *The Story of El Tejon, The Rancho and The Fort* in 1942. In 1950 she and her husband wrote *The Story of Golden Gate Park.*

Since 1943, Mrs. Giffen has been associated with The Society of California Pioneers, first as research librarian, and currently as Secretary and Editor of Publications.

Having long ago recognized the need for a bibliography of California mining town newspapers, she has devoted many years of research to its preparation. Students, historians, and those who wish to recapture the spirit of the lush times of the California mining towns will be grateful for this long overdue guide to a most exciting era of American journalism.

Hubert Howe Bancroft wrote: "The story of one mining-camp was the story of mankind; and to follow it after death was the story of the gods." Where better can one "behold the picture" than in the newspaper columns and advertisements, yellow and dingy with age, of those stirring times?

J. E. Reynolds.

Van Nuys, California,
1954.

Introduction

"ONE of the most interesting and wonderful features of California is her newspaper press . . . It has become one of the most powerful agents known among us, and holds a high and honorable rank throughout the land." So wrote the editor of the *Big Tree Bulletin*, in May, 1858.

When J. Heckendorn expressed the above opinion California's press was still in its infancy. Nevertheless, it was already exhibiting signs of becoming not only a healthy juvenile but a strong adult. The men who had come with the gold rush had as their objective the wresting of fortunes from the streams and hillsides; but they were also hungry for human companionship and news, not only local, but from home as well. They were also anxious to express their own opinions, political and otherwise, through a local press. Their rough and ready spirit found reflection in the mining town newspapers; and many a gold seeker turned editor when the opportunity offered. Gold and printer's ink mixed freely along the Mother Lode;

and even after gold had ceased to be the backbone of the communities it had built, the ink still flowed in quantity. The rattle and bang of the presses continued to shake the floors of the buildings long after the mines had lost their lure. Some of these local sheets that had their beginnings among the Long Toms and Rockers grew to maturity through the era of the Monitors and are still being published a century later.

In the columns of these early newspapers were advocated mining and land reforms that were later written into California law. Political views, especially during the days of the Lincoln-Douglas debates and the Civil War, saw newspapers established and opinions expressed that sometimes sent the editors to jail. Many an argonaut who had served his apprenticeship in the East found his way to the gold rush towns, there to lend his skill to the make-up of the local sheet. Enos Christman, the Philadelphia printer, came west in 1850, and had the honor of issuing the first edition of the *Sonora Herald*. Warren B. Ewer, John Rollin Ridge, who started Murietta on the road to fame, James Coffroth, Prentice Mulford and many others contributed their share to the literary excellence of these local publications.

Thus we find in the columns of California's early mining press an evidence of culture that the rough and ready times belied. The crucial years of the early 1860s were the incentive for some fine editorial rhetoric in support of the Union or the Confederacy as the case might be. Political repercussions throughout the world found expression in the gold rush newspapers. Many an editor, inspired by the heat of the moment, began publication of a paper that was doomed to death when its political cause was either lost or won.

The historian, the writer, the student of California's past cannot afford to overlook the columns of these early sheets. Each contains a wealth of information reflecting the local scene as well as depicting the life of that certain breed of men who left the security of their eastern homes to find fortune in an untried land.

In compiling this list it has been my aim to include not only those newspapers that had their beginnings when the magnet of the mines was drawing thousands to California, but also those that followed in the more stable days, when the railroad had made its way across the Sierra, when the placers had been worked out, the hydraulic nozzle outlawed, and the miner had taken his tools and departed for other "strikes," leaving the merchant to keep alive the towns that survived the great drama of men's greed for gold.

After some consideration as to the best way in which to present these newspapers, it was decided to list them under the town in which they were published. The localities covered are the Mother Lode, north to Weaverville and Yreka, across the Sierra to the camps of Mono and Inyo Counties, and southward to the region of Fresno and Kern Counties. This includes, so far as it has been possible to ascertain, all the mining towns in the State that had newspapers in the years 1850 to 1880.

The editors of these papers came and went as the tides of fortune rose and fell. They were the backbone of the mining press and their influence was widespread. Too much praise cannot be accorded these hardy men of the fluent pen. To their memory this history of the press of the early mining towns is dedicated.

HELEN S. GIFFEN.

San Francisco, California
1953

Table of Contents

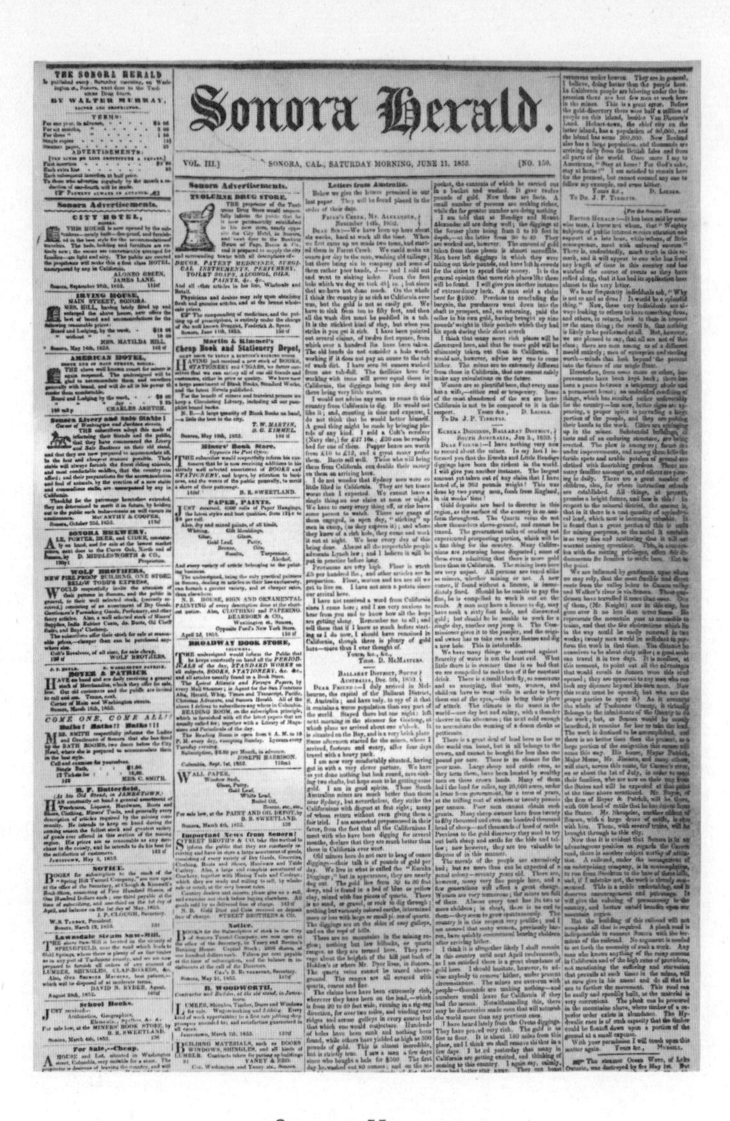

Sonora Herald.

VOL. III.] SONORA, CAL., SATURDAY MORNING, JUNE 11, 1853. [NO. 150.

Sonora Advertisements.

TUOLUMNE DRUG STORE.

Letters from Australia.

SONORA HERALD

BIG TREE BULLETIN,

AND MURPHY'S ADVERTISER.

INDEPENDENT IN ALL THINGS, NEUTRAL IN NOTHING.

VOL. 1. MAMMOTH TREE GROVE, CALAVERAS CO., CAL., FRIDAY, APRIL 30., 1858. NO. 1.

The Bulletin & Advertiser
is Published
EVERY TUESDAY AND FRIDAY,
—BY—
JOHN HECKENDORN.
Office on the stump of the Big Tree.

TERMS:

Four Months $3 00.
One Month 1 00.
Single Copy 25.
Papers supplied to Agents at $8 00 per 100 copies.

Terms of Advertising.

One square, ten lines, first insertion $3 00.
Each subsequent insertion 1 50.
N.B. To those who advertise by the month a liberal deduction will be made.

JOB PRINTING.

Having furnished our office with a new and beautiful assortment of Printing material, we are now prepared to execute every description of

PRINTING

in [illegible] workmanlike manner, at short notice, and at reasonable terms: such as

BUSINESS CARDS, CIRCULARS,
BALL TICKETS, PROGRAMMES,
LABELS, BILLS OF FARE,
BILL HEADS, CHECKS,
CERTIFICATES, SOCIETY NOTICES,
CONSTITUTIONS, BY-LAWS,
BOOKS, PAMPHLETS,
POSTERS, HANDBILLS.

PRINTING IN BRONZES AND COLORED INKS.

PROFESSIONAL CARDS.

Wm. Jones, M. D.,
PHYSICIAN & SURGEON,
MURPHY'S,
CALAVERAS CO. CALIFORNIA.
apr 30tf

E. M. Strange,
ATTORNEY AT LAW,
MURPHY'S,
CALAVERAS CO. CALIFORNIA.
apr 30tf

Francis A. Freeman,
ATT'Y & COUNSELOR AT LAW,
MURPHY'S,
CALAVERAS CO. CALIFORNIA.
apr 30tf

A. Putney,
ATT'Y AT LAW & NOTARY PUBLIC,
MURPHY'S,
CALAVERAS CO. CALIFORNIA.
apr 30tf

BUSINESS CARDS.

A. Mager,
BILLIARD SALOON,
MAIN ST., MURPHY'S,
Calaveras Co., California.
apr 30tf

Renaud & Metz,
WHOLESALE & RETAIL
DEALERS IN PROVISIONS,
Liquors, Mining Tools &c., &c.
Connected with the establishment is a Bakery where can be found at all times good Bread, Pies, Cakes, etc, etc. apr 30tf

Poetry.

TO MARY.

Here's a health to thee, Mary,
Here's a health to thee;
The drinkers are gone,
And I am alone,
To think of home and thee, Mary.

There are some who may shine o'er thee, Mary,
And many as frank, as free,
And a few as fair;
But the summer air
Is not more sweet to me, Mary.

I have thought of thy last, low sigh, Mary,
And thy dimmed and gentle eye;
And I've called on thy name
When the night winds came,
And heard my heart reply, Mary.

Be thou but true to me, Mary,
And I'll be true to thee,
And at set of sun,
When my task is done,
Be sure that I'm ever with thee, Mary.

The Trick I played upon my Wife and Aunt.

I had an aunt coming to visit me, for the first time since my marriage, and I don't know what evil genius prompted the wickedness (I acknowledge with tears in my eyes that it was such) which I perpetrated towards my wife and my ancient relative.

"My dear," said I to my wife, on the day before my aunt's arrival, "you know aunt Mary is coming to-morow; well, I forgot to mention a rather annoying circumstance with regard to her. She's very deaf, and although she can hear my voice, to which she is accustomed, in its ordinary tones, yet you will be obliged to speak extremely loud in order to be heard. It will be rather inconvenient, but I know you will do everything in your power to make her stay agreeable."

Mrs. S. announced her determination to make herself heard if possible.

I then went to John Thomas, who loves a joke as well as any person I know of, told him to be at my house at 6 P. M., on the following evening, and felt comparatively happy.

I went to the railroad station with a carriage the next evening, and when I was on my way home with my aunt, I said, "My dear aunt, there is one rather annoying infirmity that Amelia has, which I forgot to mention before. She's very deaf, and although she can hear my voice to which she is accustomed, in its ordinary tones, yet you will be obliged to speak extremely loud in order to be heard. I'm sorry for it."

Aunt Mary, in the goodness of her heart, protested that she rather liked speaking loud, and to do so would give her great pleasure.

The carriage drove up—on the steps was my wife—at the window was John Thomas, with a face as utterly solemn as if he had buried all his relatives that afternoon.

I handed out my aunt—she ascended the steps.

"I am delighted to see you," shrieked my wife, and the policeman on the other side of the street started, and my aunt nearly fell down the steps.

"[illegible]," howled my aunt; and the hall lamp clattered and the windows shook as with the fever and ague. I looked at the window—John had disappeared. Human nature could stand it no longer. I poked my head into the carriage, and went into strong convulsions.

When I entered the parlor, my wife was helping aunt Mary to take off her bonnet and crape, and there sat John with a face of woe.

Suddenly, "Did you have a pleasant journey?" went off my wife like a pistol, and John Thomas jumped to his feet.

"Rather dusty," was the response in a war-hoop, and so the conversation continued.

The neighbors for streets around must have heard it; when I was in the third story of the building, I heard every word plainly.

In the course of the evening, my aunt took occasion to say to me, "how loud your wife speaks! Don't it hurt her?"

I told her all deaf persons talked loudly, and that my wife being used to it, was not affected by the exertion, and that aunt Mary was getting along very nicely with her.

Presently my wife said softly, "Alf, how very loudly your aunt talks!"

"Yes," said I, "all deaf persons do. You're getting along with her finely; she hears every word you say." And I rather think she did.

Elated by their success at being understood, they went at it hammer and songs, till everything on the mantle-piece clattered again, and I was seriously afraid of a crowd collecting in front of the house.

But the end was near. My aunt being of an investigating turn of mind, was desirous of finding out whether the exertion of talking so loud was not injurious to my wife. So said she, in an unearthly hoot, for her voice was not so musical as it was when she was young, "does'nt talking loud strain your lungs?"

"It is an exertion," shrieked my wife.

"Then why do you do it?" was the answering scream.

"Because—because—you can't hear if I don't," squealed my wife.

"What?" said my aunt, fairly rivaling a railroad whistle this time.

I began to think it time to evacuate the premises; and looking round and seeing John gone, I stepped into the back parlor, and there he lay flat on his back, with his feet at a right angle to his body, rolling from side to side with his fists poked into his ribs, and a most agonizing expression of countenance, but not uttering a sound. I immediately and involuntarily assumed a similar attitude, and I think, that from the relative position of our boots and heads, and our attempts to restrain our laughter, apoplexy must have ensued, if a horrible groan which John gave vent to in his endeavor to repress his risibility had not betrayed our hiding-place.

In rushed my wife and my aunt, who by this time comprehended the joke, and such a scolding as I then got, I never got before, and I hope never to get again.

I know not what the end would have been, if John, in his endeavors to appear respectful and sympathetic, had not given vent to such a diabolical noise, something between a groan and a horse-laugh, that gravity was upset, and we screamed in concert.

THE LECTURING MONKEY.—Of one species which Buffon calls ouarine, "I have frequently," says [illegible]—evidently not intending [illegible] on hectors or public lecturers—"been a witness of their assemblies and deliberations. Every day, both morning and evening, the ouarines assemble in the woods to receive instructions. When all come together, one among the number takes the highest place on a tree, and makes a signal with his hand to the rest to sit round in order to hearken. As soon as he sees them placed, he begins his discourse with so loud a voice, and yet in a manner so precipitate that, to hear him at a distance, one would think that the whole company were crying out at the same time; howeaer, during that time, only one is speaking, and all the rest observe the most profound silence. When this is done, he makes a sign with the hand for the rest to reply; and at that instant they raise their voices together, until by another signal of the hand they are enjoined silence. This they as readily obey; till at last the whole assembly break up, after hearing a repetition of the same preachment.

If you are in a hurry never get behind a couple that are courting. They want to make so much of each other, that they would'nt move quick if they were going to a funeral. Get behind your jolly married folks, who have lots of children at home, if you wish to get along fast. But it is best to be a little ahead of either of them.

There is a work advertised, called "Every man a Lawyer." What a state of society!

"Well, wife, I don't see how they can send a letter on them 'ere wires, without tearing on 'em all to bits." "La, me, they don't send the paper, but they send the writing in a fluid state."

It is a singular fact that a woman cannot look from a precipice of any magnitude without becoming giddy. But what is still more singular, the giddiness departs the very moment somebody puts his arm around her waist to keep her from falling—queer, isn't it?

If you wish to be released from a rash promise of marriage breathe vows of love continually after eating onions.

BIG TREE BULLETIN, first issue.

CALIFORNIA MINING TOWN NEWSPAPERS, 1850-1880

California Mining Town Newspapers 1850-1880

ANGELS CAMP: Calaveras County.

Calaveras Mountaineer—Semi-weekly, 1872-1873.

Mountain Echo—Weekly, 1879. First issue May 5, 1879. Myron Hill Reed, editor and publisher.

AUBURN: Placer County.

Democratic Signal—1860-1861. First issue August 4, 1860. Editor R. C. Poland, followed by Joseph Scobey. Publisher S. T. Newell. A campaign paper that espoused the cause of Douglas. When the favorite was defeated Newell sold out to R. J. Steele and went to San Francisco. Steele changed the name of the paper to the *States Rights Journal* and issued the first copy August 10, 1861. It ceased publication within a few weeks.

Herald—See *Placer Herald.*

Placer Argus—Weekly, 1872. Later consolidated with *Placer County Republican.*

Placer Democratic Weekly— First issue April 1854. Lynch and Sherman, owners. Philip Lynch was the first editor and was succeeded in July 1854 by L. P. Hall, whose nickname was "Long Primer," throughout California. John Shannon succeeded Hall as editor and he afterwards established the *Visalia Delta* and became co-publisher of the *Calaveras Chronicle*. Lynch became editor of the *Placer Courier*. The *Placer Democratic Weekly* championed the cause of David C. Broderick during the bitter political campaign of 1854. When Broderick was defeated the paper had no reason to continue, and ceased publication saying "it would not pay." It was succeeded by the *Auburn Whig* and that, in turn, by the *Placer Press*.

Placer Herald—Weekly, 1852. First issue September 11, 1852. Publishers, Tabb Mitchell, Richard Rust and John McElroy. Size of paper 14″x20″, 20 columns. Issued on Saturdays. The opening editorial proclaimed the paper "free and independent," but it soon took on a strong Democratic flavor and wielded considerable power in that party. In the fall of 1852, Tabb Mitchell bought out his partners and in December of 1852 Charles Mitchell took over an interest, with Tabb remaining as editor. September 1853, Charles retired and the paper was enlarged to 6 columns to a page, 22″ in length. In January 1856 James Anderson purchased a one-third interest and became editor; but in April 1857 Charles Mitchell once more became actively interested, taking over Anderson's share. In 1859 the *Herald* engaged in a lively political controversy with the Republicans; but after Lincoln's assassination it eased its attitude and carried the sombre black border of national mourning. William H. Smith leased it in 1867 and Lieutenant Governor Joseph Walkup became its editor. In 1868 Walkup took over under the name of Walkup and Company with Robert Hartley and William Smith as his partners. 1872, James A. Filcher became a partner with Walkup, still editor, a post he held until his death in the *Herald* office, October 15, 1873. This left Filcher in control. There were a number of lessees following, among them W. A. Shepard who went to work on the paper in 1889 and purchased it from Filcher in 1900.

Placer Press—(succeeded by *Whig*) June 1855-1858. South and Company, publishers; T. W. Scobey, editor. Supported the cause of the Know-Nothing, or American Party. Hiram R. Hawkins, A. L. Stimson, Charles Winkley became owners with Hawkins editor.

Stars and Stripes — Weekly, 1863-1872. First issue July 29, 1863. Published by J. C. Boggs, with W. A. Selkirk as editor. It was the first Republican paper in Placer County. Size 14″x20″, 24 columns. Three pages of the first issue were devoted exclusively to advertising. Published every Wednesday. During the years of its life it had many changes of editors and publishers. Selkirk retired as editor in February 1864, and returned in August of 1865, only to withdraw again, the following November. Boggs retired in 1866 and Ed. C. Littlefield became editor. In 1867 Selkirk returned to buy out Boggs' interest and assume editorship. Hart Fellows bought out Selkirk in 1867, becoming editor. Fellows was owner and editor in 1869. In 1872 the paper backed Horace Greeley; and it ceased publication November 28, 1872.

States Rights Journal—See *Democratic Signal.*

Union Advocate—1861-1863? James P. Bull, manager; Hiram Hawkins, editor.

Whig—First issue October 21, 1854. C. Walkley, A. D. Stimson, owners; M. E. Mills, editor. This paper had 31 issues with Mills as editor for the first three months. Hawkins succeeded him and served until the final issue May 19, 1855.

BENTON: Mono County.

Bentonian—Semi-weekly, tri-weekly, weekly, 1879-1880?

Mono Weekly Messenger—February-April 1879.

BIDWELL'S BAR: Butte County.

Weekly Butte Record — November 12, 1855-June 1856. George H. Crosette, editor. Moved to Oroville, June 28, 1856.

BIG TREE GROVE: Calaveras County.

Big Tree Bulletin and Murphy's Advertiser—Published semi-weekly, April-July 1858. First issue April 30, 1858, last issue July 3, 1858, sixteen issues in all. The final issue was published at Murphy's. J. Heckendorn was the editor and publisher. The press was set up in the open air on the stump of the giant Sequoia. Its motto was "Independent in all things, neutral in none." The editorial of the first issue said: "To-day for the first time in the period of the world's history we issue a paper, the office of which is established upon a stump. It will be the object of our little sheet to give detailed accounts of the country . . ." Owing to falling off of patronage in the Mammoth Tree Grove the paper did not prosper, and on Saturday, July 3, 1858 the final edition was put out from Murphy's, the editor announcing that he was going to the mines if the local people would not support his publication. Since there were no more issues, J. Heckendorn must have carried out his threat.

BODIE: Mono County.

Chronicle—Weekly and daily, 1863-1880. Also known as *Alpine Chronicle*, published in Markleeville, Alpine County. United with *Bridgeport Union* to become *Bridgeport Chronicle-Union*, and published in Bridgeport Dec. 1878. Still published.

Free Press—Weekly, daily, 1879-1885. First distributed as a throw-away advertising paper.

Morning News—Daily, March 1879-June 20, 1880. United with *Bodie Standard* to become *Bodie Standard-News.*

BRIDGEPORT: Mono County.

Chronicle-Union—See *Bodie Chronicle.*

COLOMA: El Dorado County.

El Dorado News—July 19-Dec. 6, 1851. Moved to Placerville and discontinued in 1853. T. A. Springer and F. H. Harman, publishers and editors. A Whig paper.

Empire County Argus—1853-1857. John Conness and T. M. Reed, owners; N. W. Fuller, editor. Printed in Coloma on presses purchased from the *Miner's Advocate* of Diamond Springs. It was Democratic in political view, favoring Senator David C. Broderick. D. P. Tallmage succeeded N. W. Fuller as editor. He held this post until the end of 1855 when W. J. Forbes and C. Woods took the paper over. They continued to publish until they failed, the last issue being November 1856. This left Coloma without a newspaper. The citizens took up a collection and made good the paper's debts and publication was resumed until July 23, 1857, when H. S. Smith and Company purchased it and moved it to Placerville where it appeared August 13, 1857 as the *Tri-Weekly Argus*. This in turn was succeeded by the *Tri-Weekly Index*, Lanyard and Phelps publishers, *Tri-Weekly Register*, *Semi-Weekly Register*, *Semi-Weekly Observer*. The latter discontinued in February, 1860.

Miner's Advocate—1852. Also published in Diamond Springs. First issue in the summer of 1852. Edited by S. Garfield and D. W. Gelwicks. James R. Pile and Company were the owners. In 1853 the paper and its presses were purchased by John Conness and T. M. Reed who, in the summer of 1853, began the publishing of the *Empire County Argus*.

True Republican—First issue October, 1857. Wheelock, Kies and Cole were owners and editors. The firm dissolved in 1858 and the paper was taken over by George O. Kies.

COLUMBIA: Tuolumne County.

Columbian Citizen—Weekly, 1867. Published by W. G. Dinsmore.

Columbia Clipper — Weekly. May 1854-May 1857. Heckendorn, Gist and Wilson, owners. J. Heckendorn, editor. An organ of the Know-Nothing Party. See *Columbia Gazette*.

Columbia Gazette—Weekly, semi-weekly, November 1852-1858. Colonel T. A. Falconer, founder and editor.

This was the second paper published in Columbia. It was independent in politics for a short time and then swung to the Democratic standard. In 1853, Col. Falconer retired and J. C. and W. A. Duchow became the editors, joined by P. M. Lancey. In 1854 the paper was issued as the *Clipper and Gazette.* Lancey remained until November 1855 when the paper was merged with the *Southern Mines Advertiser*, a semi-weekly publication edited by T. N. Cazneau and J. C. Duchow until July 1856, at which time Duchow leased the paper for six months. In the winter and spring of 1858, J. W. Oliver was editor and the paper was anti-administration in sentiment. It was the first of the Columbia papers to swing to the support of Douglas. Oliver was succeeded as editor by G. R. Parburt, and within a few weeks of his association with it, the paper died a natural death.

Columbia News — August, 1858. Edited by D. Youcham.

Columbia Star—Weekly, October 28, 1851-November 1, 1851. The first paper published in Columbia. It was printed on the old Ramage press from the *Sonora Herald*, which had been purchased by G. W. Gore, publisher and editor of the *Star*. It is said that the first issue off the press was purchased by a Mrs. deNoielle, first woman resident of Columbia, who had crossed the plains. She paid an ounce of gold dust for the paper. It is possible that James

Coffroth worked on this newspaper for a short time after leaving the *Sonora Herald*. Gore got into financial trouble and Lewis Gunn sued him for the balance due on the Ramage. In order to satisfy the debt the press was sold at auction, Gunn bidding it in. It was placed in the street in front of the *Star* office awaiting transportation to Sonora. The night of November 13, 1851, the press was set on fire, presumably by the disgruntled Gore and his associates.

Columbia Times—Weekly, 1860-61.

Columbian Weekly—June 1856-May, 1857. First issue June 21, 1856. Edited by J. M. Oliver, with a circulation of over one thousand, which was the largest distribution of any newspaper in the southern mines.

Tuolumne Courier—Issued from the office of the *Columbian Weekly*. First issued June 20, 1856. Editors and publishers, William A. and J. C. Duchow and J. B. Urmy. Purchased Feb. 18, 1864 by George Sharrats and moved to Sonora. Suspended publication July 16, 1866.

COPPER CITY: Shasta County.

Pioneer—Weekly, published April 1864-May 1866, by W. L. Carter. Suspended publication, 1866.

COPPEROPOLIS: Calaveras County.

Courier—April 1865-1867? Published by Ransom and Benham.

DARWIN: Inyo County.

Coso Mining News—Weekly, 1875-1878. T. S. Harris, editor. When Harris moved from Panamint to Darwin it took almost a week to transport his printing office over the rugged roads. First issue of the *Coso Mining News* Nov. 6, 1875. Last issue Sept. 4, 1878. The materials of the paper were sent to Bodie where it was merged with the *Standard.* In the 1880s Harris started a newspaper in Santa Ana and later he went to Lancaster, where he began the *Lancaster Weekly News.* In the first month of 1884 he became involved in a quarrel with the editor of the *Evening Republican* of Los Angeles, and this ended in the shooting, by Harris, of the editor, Charles Whitehead. A prison sentence followed for Harris, and he finally committed suicide in November of 1893.

DIAMOND SPRINGS: El Dorado County.

El Dorado County Journal—Weekly, Jan. 1-29, 1856.

Miner's Advocate—Also published in Coloma. First issue in summer of 1852, in Coloma. When the paper's press was purchased by John Conness and T. M. Reed in the summer of 1853, it was used to print the *Empire County Argus.* The paper removed to Coloma, where Fred A. Snyder was editor, until July 23, 1854. Snyder came across the plains to California in 1849, and was a member of the California Legislature in the session of 1852-1853. During a visit to Lake Bigler (Tahoe) in July of 1854 he was drowned. The following year the paper was purchased by Doctor Bradley of Placerville, who moved it and changed the name to the *El Dorado County Journal*.

DOUGLAS CITY (TRINITY RANCH): Trinity County.
Trinity Gazette—Weekly, 1861-1862.

DOWNIEVILLE: Sierra County.
Bugle—Published in the fall of 1852 and printed on the *Echo* press by W. S. Spear, editor. It was a Whig paper and was published only during the political campaign of 1852.

Democrat—Weekly, May 1870-May 1871.

Mountain Echo—1851-1854. Became the *Sierra Citizen* in 1854. W. T. Giles was editor and owner. The paper first published in the spring of 1851 was the first newspaper in Downieville. The press had to be brought into the town on skids. It was Democratic in sentiment. In 1852 it was taken over by King, Wright and Ham. During the winter of 1852-53 a severe storm caused a paper shortage and it became necessary to print the news on wrapping paper. In the spring of 1853 both political views and ownership changed. Oscar Bull became editor, and in the summer of 1854, the name was changed to the *Sierra Citizen.*

Mountain Messenger — Published in Downieville 1853-1854. See Gibsonville *Herald* and La Porte *California Mountain Messenger.*

Old Oaken Bucket—A weekly temperance paper from July 4, 1855 to the fall of the same year. George E. Talmadge and Calvin B. McDonald, publishers.

Sierra Advocate — Weekly, June 1866-August 1867. Published in 1867 by J. H. Dormer.

Sierra County News—Weekly, March to September 1862.

Sierra Democrat — Weekly, June 1856-1864. See *Georgetown Weekly News.* Published first in Forest City, eight miles from Downieville. It was moved to Downieville within a year of the first issue. While in Forest City the owner was John Platt and the editor W. Campbell. When the paper moved it retained the same owner, and W. J. Forbes was the editor and part owner. January 1, 1858, the plant was destroyed by fire, and in order not to lose their subscribers the paper was kept alive by printing advertising slips on the press of the *Mountain Messenger.* A new press was purchased in Sacamento and heavy snows raised the transportation charges to $400. In 1863 John B. Reed became associated with the *Democrat;* but the plant burned again in February, 1864 and the salvaged materials were purchased by Dewey and Vaughan.

Standard — Semi-weekly, 1863-1864. Matt Lynch, publisher. Formerly known as *Weekly Standard* of Quincy. Moved to Downieville April 6, 1864. Ceased publication in October, 1864.

DUTCH FLAT: Placer County.

Enquirer—Weekly, semi-weekly, 1860-1868. E. B. Boust, publisher. The paper was started after Boust left the Iowa Hill *Patriot*. It proved a flourishing sheet for a number of years. When the Central Pacific by-passed Dutch Flat, it ceased publication.

Forum — October, 1875. Changed name to *Placer Times*, which was a weekly, 1881.

FOLSOM (also known as NEGRO BAR): Sacramento County.

Granite Journal—March 8, 1856. Printed on the press used by the *Diamond Springs Advocate*. First published and edited by L. Bradley and S. Seabough. Sold to George H. Baker. See Granite, Sacramento County.

Folsom Dispatch—1856-1858. Weekly. Carpenter and Wellington, publishers; W. Ewing, editor. 1858, W. Penry and Co., publishers.

Folsom Telegraph—Weekly, 1856-?

FOREST CITY: Sierra County.

Sierra Democrat — See Downieville *Sierra Democrat.* and Georgetown *Weekly News.*

Sierra Free Press—August 6-Dec. 1880.

FOREST HILL: Placer County.

Courier—See Yankee Jim's *Placerville Courier.*

FORT JONES: Siskiyou County.

Scott Valley News—Semi-weekly, 1878-? Published by B. H. Evans. In 1879 Evans sold to Norcross and Curtis. In 1880 E. S. Culver became associated with it and it was independent in politics, and filled with local news.

Scott Valley Mirror — 1860. Dr. D. M. Davidson started this paper on an old hand press brought from Yreka's *Mountain Herald*, in 1860. The publication lasted a year and was then purchased by Dumont and Fowler and taken to Yreka where it became the *National Democrat*, supporting Breckenridge in opposition to Douglas.

GEORGETOWN: El Dorado County.

Gazette—Founded April 9, 1880 by Horace W. Hulbert and inherited by his daughter, Maud, who became editor at sixteen years of age and who carried on the paper for a generation.

Butte Record.

VOLUME 2. BIDWELL, BUTTE COUNTY, CALIFORNIA, SEPTEMBER 22, 1855. NUMBER 48.

Poet's Corner.

Will You Love Me When I am Old?

Will Affection still enfold me,
As the day of life declines,
When Old Age, with ruthless vigor,
[illegible]

When the eye forgets its seeing,
And the hand forgets its skill,
When the weary words prove rebels
To the Mind's once kindly will:

When the deaf ear, strained to listen,
Scarcely hears the opening word,
And th' unfathomed depths of feeling
Are by no swift currents stirred:

When fond Memory like a limner,
Many a line perspective casts,
Spreading out our by gone pleasures
On the canvas of the Past:

When the leaping blood grows sluggish,
And the fire of youth had fled,
When the friends who now surround us
Half are numbered with the dead:

When the years begin to shorten,
Scarcely leaving us a trace,
When Old Time, with bold approaches,
Marks his dial on my face:

When our present hopes, all gathered,
Lie like dead flowers on our track,
When the whole of our existence
Is one fearful looking-back:

When each wasted hour of talent,
Scarcely measured now at all,
Sends its witness back to haunt us,
Like the writing on the wall:

When the ready tongue is palsied,
And the form is bowed with care,
When our only hope is Heaven,
And our only help is prayer:

When our idols, broken round us,
Fall amid the ranks of men,
Until Death uplifts the curtain,
Will thy Love endure till then?

The oracle spoke the truth. The Prince Albert was destined never to complete her voyage. On the third day of the passage out a storm arose that drove the schooner upon one of the low coral islets that stud the Antilles. Our author thus, with pen and [illegible] forth the shipwreck:

"A sound, hoarse and steady, but louder even than that of the wind, broke on our ears. It was evident that we were approaching it, for every instant it became more distinct and ominous. I gazed ahead into the hopeless darkness, when suddenly a broad sheet of lightning revealed immediately before us, and not a cable's length distant, what, under the lurid gleam, appeared to be a wall of white spray, dashing literally a hundred feet in the air—a hell of waters, from which there was no escape. "El Roncador!" shrieked the captain, in a voice of utter despair, that even then thrilled like a knife in my heart. The fearful moment of death had come, and I had barely time to draw a full breath of preparation for the struggle, when we were literally whelmed in the raging waters. I felt a shock, a sharp jerk, and the hiss and gurgle of the sea, a sensation of immense pressure, followed by a blow like that of a heavy fall. Again I was lifted up, and again struck down, but this time with less force. I had just enough consciousness left to know that I was striking on the sand, and I made an involuntary effort to rise and escape from the waves. Before I could gain my feet I was again struck down, again and again, until nearer dead than alive, I at last succeeded in crawling to a spot where the water did not reach me. I [illegible] it into execution, he presented a truly American argument to the contrary, in the shape of a revolver. They attempted to flee; but the captain was caught, and the muzzle of the pistol [illegible] unpleasantly close to his [illegible] in the most abject terms; and was finally released on condition of carrying the party from the island. To make sure that he should not give them the slip, he was obliged to take up his residence in the hut, while his men remained on board the vessel. The mysterious revolver was as potent as a magician's wand in keeping the worthy captain under due subjection; and in course of time he began to entertain quite a liking for his peremptory hosts; so much so, that on reaching his village, after leaving El Roncador, he manifested his high respect for them by getting up a dance in their honor. The music for the entertainment consisted of a violin, two guitars, and a queer Indian instrument consisting of a perforated gourd over which were strained brass wires in lieu of strings. The refreshment consisted of Jamaica rum, flavored with the juice of the sugar cane, lemons, and red pepper. Everybody got gloriously drunk, quarreled, broke their instruments over each others heads, then cried, embraced and became good friends again. And so the entertainment came to an end.

The tortoise hunting on El Roncador had been so successful, that our artist put a few hundred dollars in his purse by the sale of the shell which he had collected. So with renewed courage he embarked for the Mosquito capital.

The royal residence is described by

and dead, from 'Pompey' down to 'Wellington.'"

Walking out the morning after his arrival, Mr. Bard encountered a tall [illegible] serious looking white man, who invited him to his house. It was a [illegible] building of rough boards, [illegible] number of small rooms opening into a larger one. All around were hung portraits of the Queen of England. A sleepy looking black girl, with an enormous head of frizzled hair, was lazily sweeping the floor, as they entered. Little did our wanderer dream of the august presence into which he was soon to be ushered.

'At a word from the gentleman,' says the narrative, "the torpid black girl disappeared for a few moments, and then came back with some cups and a pot of coffee. I observed that there were three cups, and that my host filled them all, which I thought a little singular, since there were but two of us. A faint, momentary suspicion crossed my mind, that the female polypus stood in some such relation to my host as to warrant her in honoring us with her company. But, instead of doing so, she unceremoniously pushed open a door in the corner, and curtly ejaculated to some unseen occupant, 'Get up!' There was a kind of querulous response, and directly a thumping and muttering, as of some person who regarded himself as unreasonably disturbed. Meanwhile we had each finished our first cup of coffee, and were proceeding with a second, when the door in the corner opened, and a black boy, or what an American would be apt to call a 'a young darkey,' apparently nineteen or twenty years old, shuffled up to the table. He wore only a shirt, un-

of a man of middle age, much emaciated, and horribly disfigured by what is called the bulpis, a species of syphilitic leprosy, which is almost universal on the coast, and which, with the aid of rum, has already reduced the population to one half [illegible] This disgusting disease is held in such terror by the Indians of the interior, that they have prohibited all sexual relations between their people and the Sambos of the coast, under the penalty of death.

"Around the pitpan were stationed a number of women, with palm branches, to keep off the flies, which swarmed around the already festering corpse.—Their frizzled hair started from their heads like the snakes on the brow of the fabled Gorgon, and they swayed their bodies to and fro, keeping a kind of treadmill step to the measure of the doleful tum-tum. With the exception of the men who beat the drum and blew the pipe, these women appeared to be the only persons at all interested in the proceedings. The rest were standing in groups, or squatted at the roots of the palm-trees. I was beginning to get tired of the performance, when, with a suddenness which startled even the women around the corpse, four men, entirely naked excepting a cloth wrapped round their loins, and daubed over with variously colored clays, rushed from the interior of one of the huts, and hastily fastening a piece of rope to the half of the pitpan containing the corpse, dashed away toward the woods, dragging it after them, like a sledge. The women with the Gorgon heads, and the men with the drum and trumpet, followed them on the run, each keeping time on his respective

their intrigues. They pitched, for monarch, upon a drunken Sambo "who combined," according to the reports of their own agents, "all the bad qualities of the European and the Creole, with the vicious propensities of the Sambo and the [illegible] of the Indian." The [illegible] of this interesting [illegible] was short. He was killed, in 1824, in a drunken brawl, and was succeeded by his half-brother Robert. But the new king was not to the liking of his protectors, who deposed him, and put in his place another Sambo, who was crowned under the name of George Frederick. His reign was also brief; and he was succeeded by another Sambo, Robert Charles Frederick, who was solemnly crowned at Belize on the 23d of April, 1825.

There is extant an account of the ceremonial, which is intensely ludicrous. The monarch was dressed in the uniform of a British major, his court mostly wore sailors' trowsers, some with shirts, and some without. His majesty seemed chiefly occupied in admiring his finery; and after the anointing oil, which was highly perfumed, had been poured upon his head, he expressed his delight at this portion of the ceremony by repeatedly passing his hands through his bushy locks, and then applying them to his nose. Preparatory to taking the oath of allegiance, "upon the faith of a Christian, it was necessary that they should profess Christianity. They were accordingly baptized. After this solemn mockery they all proceeded to get beastly drunk at the coronation dinner which was provided for them.

But his sable Majesty proved somewhat refractory, and his protectors re-

'When I had got near him, he adjusted himself in position, and compressed his lips, with an affectation of [illegible] dignity. Hardly able to restrain laughing outright, I took off my hat, and saluted him with a profound bow, and [illegible] but the strain was too great [illegible] remaining button of his waistband: It gave way, and, to borrow a [illegible] phrase, the nether garment 'came down on the run!' The captain, however, no way disconcerted, gathered it up with both hands, and held it in place, while I read the 'paper that talked.'"

The Raining Tree.—The island of Fierro is one of the most considerable of the Canaries, and I conceive the name to be given it upon this account—that, its soil not affording so much as a drop of fresh water, seems to be iron, and indeed in this island there is neither a river or rivulet, nor well or spring, save that only toward the seaside there are some wells, but they lie at such a distance from the city that the inhabitants can make no use thereof. But the great Preserver and Sustainer of all remedies this inconvenience, by a way so extraordinary, that man will be forced to sit down and acknowledge that He gives in this an undeniable demonstration of His wonderful goodness. For in the midst there is a tree, which is the only one of the kind, insomuch as it has no resemblance to any of those known to us in Europe. The leaves of it are long and narrow, and continue in constant verdure, winter and summer, and its branches are covered with a cloud which is never dis-

Butte Record, when published from Bidwell's Bar.

Folsom Dispatch.

VOL. 2. FOLSOM, SACRAMENTO CO., CAL., SATURDAY, FEBRUARY 6, 1858. NO. 19.

The Folsom Dispatch
IS PUBLISHED EVERY SATURDAY BY
G. E. WELLINGTON & CO.
GEO. E. WELLINGTON. WM. M. PERRY.

TERMS—INVARIABLY IN ADVANCE.

Per Annum	$4 00
Six months	2 50
Three months	1 50
Single copies	12½
Advertising per square first insertion	2 00
Each subsequent insertion	1 50

Liberal deductions on business cards, and other quarterly advertising.

JOB PRINTING of every description executed in a superior manner, and at low prices.

Business Cards.

Drs Donaldson & Bates,
—OFFICE AT—
Corner of Sutter and Wool streets,
n6-tf. FOLSOM.

Dr. S. Lyons.
Physician & Surgeon
Office on Sutter st. opposite Patterson's Hotel

Dr. J. R. Dutin,
Physician & Surgeon
Office in Uniontown, El Dorado Co.

Dentistry done in scientific manner and at low rates.

S. F. Marquis, M. D.,
Physician & Surgeon
TENDERS his professional services to the citizens of Granite City and vicinity. Particular attention given to private diseases, and a cure warranted in all cases where his directions are followed.
Office next door to Magnolia Saloon D catur street.
Also Justice of the Peace

H. B. Meredith,
NOTARY PUBLIC.
Office on Leidesdorff street.
n6t Folsom, May, 9th, 1857

G. M. COLE.
ATTORNEY and COUNSELLOR
AT LAW.
Particular attention given to conveyancing and Surveying. Office—Sutter st., near the Post Office. Folsom April 4th 1857–1q

POETRY.

There are some things which escape the fangs of criticism while others are pilfered and destroyed in beauty and harmony by the plagiarist. We find the following atrocious parody circulating in the newspapers without credit. Perhaps it was written by Miss Phebe Carey, who has a talent for such kind of performances; at all events, it is "well done." But isn't it rather too bad to parody such a beautiful poem as is "Annabel Lee," (published in a previous paper.)—though [illegible] can help [illegible] at this thing after all:

DEBORAH LEE.

BY FUZZY GUZZY.

'Tis a dozen or so years ago,
Somewhere in the West countree,
That a nice girl lived, as the Hosiers know,
By the name of Deborah Lee.
Her sister was loved by Edgar Poe,
But Deborah by me! Ah me-e.e.

Now I was green, and she was green,
As a summer squash might be;
But we loved as warmly as other folks,
I and Deborah Lee! You see?
With a love that the lasses of Hoosierdom
Coveted her and me.

But somehow it happened long ago,
In the aguish West countree,
That a chill March morning gave the "shakes"
To my beautiful Deborah Lee;
And the grim Steam Doctor (curse him!) came
And bore her away from me;
The Doctor and Death—old partners they,
In the aguish West countree.

The angels wanted her up in Heaven,
[But they never asked for "me!"]
And that is the reason, I rather guess,
In the aguish West countree,
That the cold March wind and the Doctor and Death
Took off my Deborah Lee,
My beautiful Deborah Lee,
From the warm sunshine and the opening flowers,
And laid her away from me.

Our love was as strong as a six-mule team,
Or the love of folks older than we,
But Death, with the aid of Doctor and steam,
Was rather too many for me;
[illegible]

ant expression as though challenging some imaginary biped of the male species. Nellie, as if to accept the challenge for the absent sex, planted a kiss upon the cheek of Louise, and then glided away to give vivacity to another part of the house.

Brother Bill by this time had scented the flavor of breakfast, and having decided proclivities for the good things of the table, made essay to deliver himself from dreamland and at last succeeded in plasting himself within his habiliaments he descended the stairway, and was met by a "Happy New Year" from his active brother, Ned, who had conspired with Nellie to take him unawares.

By this time the married folks began to appear, and they ascertained that in spite of their advantage of experience, and in contradiction to their own teachings, the young folks were too smart for them. This was particularly annoying to Tom and Carrie, who had a short time previous, formed an alliance for better or worse, which arrangement Nellie proved to be a retrograde movement from the fact of their apparent total ignorance of a new year having been born, until advised of it, and their finding themselves indebted to the amount of numerous forfeits.

The first breakfast of that year was a happy one to all assembled beneath that hospitable roof. Upon the countenance of that family there radiated a smile resembling the lingering of a summer's day among the grey annals of winter.

Nellie bestowed many a bewitching, coaxing glance among the younger members, and she annoyed brother Bill by making him speak when he was particularly occupied with causing the disappearance of numerous substantial dishes, from the table.

Breakfast was succeeded by a great amount of merriment and illuminated fun and frolic, and in triumphant joy the day sped on.

"Oh, here comes Abbie F. and her beau!" cried Nellie, as in an advanced hour of the day they stood at the window coquettishly humming a merry tune, which out of compliment to her sentimental cousin, whom she was endeavoring to make tread the measure, she called the "rogue's march."

"Now we will have lots of fun," said Nellie—"I wish I had a beau!—how I would tease him."

"Perhaps he would tease you," mischievously remarked sister Frances, who, having the advantage of Nellie in years, was supposed to know more of the ways of the opposite sex.

Nellie looked skeptical at the idea of any one outflirting her, and forgetting [illegible] replete with the beautiful and the brave. Nellie, natural as a fawn and bewitching in every movement, darted around her shafts of pointed wit, and occasionally an arrow from cupid's bow.

The promenade succeeded during the cessation of the music. Abbie had wandered from her partner, and stood gazing on the likeness of a Californian who had been long absent.

"Ah, I have caught you!" exclaimed Nellie, as she approached to where Abbie stood, ever thinking of the distant one. "But," she added, "they say he declares himself in opposition to all that is feminine, and I am prepared to believe him a perfect skeptic to there existing in the composition of our sex, aught that is good. And they say, too, that he smokes pipes of horrid tobacco, like all other Californians! and for my part I'll think no more of him. And away Nellie glided, humming the tune—"No man's wife I'll be!"

Abbie glanced at her receding form and murmured—"I care not if he does smoke that horrid weed, as Nellie calls it, and even if he does wear moustaches—I don't think them so very ugly—and I am sure had he not been brave, he would never have gone to that country so young; and," she continued, "I wish he had not gone there."

"So do I, Abbie," remarked Frances, who had entered unobserved. "I am his sister, and like you, I wish he were here to-night, and I believe he will return, if not with accumulated gold, with a heart of diamond, unsullied by contact with the world. So let us hope, at least," added Frances. "Now, let us join the company.

Lightly the hours passed by within those festive halls, for the gayest of the gay were assembled there. At last the small hours of morning appeared, and the music ceased. The sound of sleigh bells were again heard and the guests began to take their departure for home. There was an immense amount of kissing among the females, while their gallants looked wistfully on the operation, murmuring that they could not share the entertainment.

After the last good-by had been said, the family circled round the fire to congratulate each other that the new year had commenced under such pleasant auspices.

The boys, headed by brother Bill, were noticed to absent themselves, and return with a mischievous smile on their countenances.

At a late hour the family retired. Nellie proceeded to her room which she entered but had no sooner done so, than she uttered a piercing scream and fled the apartment. [illegible]

ORIGINAL.

ON DRUNKEN SPREES.

It is perfectly natural and reasonable for any man, after he has once became intoxicated, to continue so for some time, as is generally the case with drinking men.—The reason is that when a man has an intoxicated mind, that same mind is what he is to choose his course with; hence, if his mind is wrong and foolish he will decide to foolishly take [illegible] liquor to make him still more foolish, and the more foolish his foolish mind gets the more foolishness that incompetent mind will guide him to do. We ask why an insane man raves and gnaws his own flesh? The answer is easy: his mind is defective and so directs him, and that same defective mind is all the guide he has. In like manner, is it any wonder that a man, after he is perfectly saturated and pickled with brandy, knows any better than to keep himself so? It is as natural for drinking men to drink by sprees as it is for every man to act according to the mind he possesses, and the legitimate end of a spree is what some call *delirium* "*tremendous;*" and instead of wondering why drinking men don't get sober, we wonder why their drunken minds don't decide for them to keep drunk as long as it has any care drowning force. But the matter which most astonishes us is how a sober sensible man who knows what has often befallen him while in sprees, who knows that in each spree he has had for years, he has spent all the money he had and all he could borrow, lost much of his property and his friends, let every wag who saw fit make an ass of him, can get drunk. We say, to see these kind of men deliberately drink, is what astonishes us. We know arsenic would poison us and we are most afraid to handle it to kill rats. The encounters some men have with liquor, in sprees, comes so near being what death would be to us, that we wonder they do not fear liquor as we do arsenic. The soldier who would run when bullets were whistling or who would sleep on his watch, might deserve blame, but the sentinel who, [illegible]

Poverty and Pride.

M. de Prony inhabited one of the most populous and unwholesome quarters of the capital, in the neighborhood of the Place Maubert. Every morning as he went out at day-break, he was accustomed to meet an old man and woman, arm in arm, walking slowly, and carrying, the one in the right hand and the other in the left hand, a red-herring by a string. It was the [illegible] the time of the Regence; they had infatuated themselves with their sumptuosity, and revolutions had ruined them "*des pieds a la tete.*" For the space of four years M. de Prony daily witnessed the feast of these two octogenarians; they had such a great look of dignity in their misfortune, that he never dared offer them the least token of his interest and esteem. Prony was absent for several months. He returned to Paris and took to his same apartments and habits. But how great was his grief, when he descended his staircase, for the first time, to behold the old woman alone clinging to the banisters, and holding but a single herring this time; suddenly he stumbled against something in the dark, which had remained unperceived.

"I crave pardon," exclaimed a feeble and tremulous voice; "do not stir sir—pray wait an instant."

"Why so?"

"You would prevent me from dining."

"I do not understand you."

"Ah! you would, perhaps, trample on a fine red-herring that I have just bought, and chanced to let fall."

"I will help you," said Prony, "if you will allow me."

The professor sought more with his hands than with his eyes, for the dinner of the man of Regence; he, at length, found it, and in restoring it, said to him:

"The little service which I have rendered to you is fortunate, for by the side of your heraing is a well-filled purse, which you must also have dropped; and, judging by the sound of it, it is gold."

"This purse does not belong to me," an- [illegible]

FOLSOM DISPATCH, 1858, carried masthead of the Folsom Railroad, forerunner of the Central Pacific.

Gem—First issue April 12, 1872. Owned and edited by E. L. Crawford: Ceased April 6, 1877.

Weekly News—October 18, 1854-May 22, 1856. Merged with Forest City *Sierra Democrat* in 1856. J. W. Oliver, first editor and publisher; Feb. 1855, Theo. Platt, Jr., owner, Oliver, editor; May 1855, J. G. McCallum became editor and partner; Nov. 1855, Platt and Shaw, owners.

GIBSONVILLE: Sierra County.

Herald—1853-1855. See La Porte *Mountain Messenger*. First editor and owner a Mr. Heade, who was succeeded in 1854 by Alfred Helm, who issued a supplement called the *St. Louis News*, which was delivered in St. Louis, Missouri, by special messenger. In 1855 the paper was sold and taken to La Porte to become the *Mountain Messenger*. Early issues were destroyed by fire.

Trumpet—1854-1855, Helm and Myers, publishers. See *Mountain Messenger*.

GRANITE: Sacramento County.

Granite Journal—1856. Published every Wednesday by George H. Baker, who had been associated with the *Spirit of the Age*, in Sacramento. In December 1855 he turned his attention to the *Granite Journal* after disposing of his Sacramento interests. The paper only lasted a year.

Baker was better known as a lithographer than as a journalist. His "Birdseye View of Sacramento, City of the Plains," designed and published in 1857, is one of his most valuable productions.

GRASS VALLEY: Nevada County.

Daily National Gazette — See Grass Valley *Nevada National Weekly.*

Foothill Weekly—From January 1874-? Titles varied: *Tidings, Telegraph.*

Mining Journal—July 1865-?

Nevada National Weekly — 1855-1872. Edited by Rufus Shoemaker from 1855-1859. From September to November 26, 1859, edited by J. H. Boardman. 1860, C. S. Wells and Company, owners; C. F. Smith, editor. Warren B. Ewer became editor in 1861, succeeding Smith. Under Ewer it became a tri-weekly publication. In 1862 the paper again changed hands, with W. S. Byrne and J. P. Skelton buying an interest, and Byrne assuming the editorship. June 11, 1862 the plant was destroyed by fire and publication was not resumed until July 19. In 1863 Ewer sold his interest to Wells, and John Rollin Ridge bought a quarter interest and became co-editor with Byrne. August 1864, the paper made its appearance as a daily, the first in Grass Valley. In April 1865, Wells bought out Byrne and the firm was known as the National Printing

Company with Wells, Ridge and Skelton as owners; Ridge as editor. Ridge died in 1867 and the paper ceased publication in 1872.

Republican—Daily, Nov. 9, 1871-April 9, 1872. D. B. Frink, publisher and owner. Removed to Truckee where it became the *Truckee Republican.*

Telegraph—First issue September 1853. Oliver and Moore, proprietors. In May 1854 Warren B. Ewer and J. H. Boardman took over, with H. J. Shipley as editor. The latter was a brilliant editor, but he ran into the temperament of the notorious Lola Montez, and because of fancied insults she gave him a public whipping that ended his editorial career in Grass Valley. He left, and after spending some time in Nevada City and Sacramento he died in the latter city by his own hand. In 1854 the paper office burned and again, in July 1855 of that year, it was taken over by Rufus Shoemaker and George D. Roberts, and the name was changed to the *Nevada National Weekly*, published in Grass Valley, but distributed from Nevada City.

Union — Began publication October 1864, supporting the re-election of President Lincoln and opposing the stand of John Rollin Ridge, editor of the *Nevada National.* The men behind the financing of the Union were not known, and the only name openly associated with its editorial staff was that of James W. E. Townsend, a wandering editor who served a journalistic career in Virginia City, Bodie, and other far flung mining towns. He was known as "Lyin' Jim" and during his career on the *Union* he is said to have taken the paper forms to the *National* office in the dead of night, and almost caused the *Union's* death. Someone was in on the plot, and the forms were retrieved and the paper was issued on time, but Townsend was forced to leave the vicinity. H. C. Bennett became editor, and Ridge of the *National* once challenged the supposed head of the *Union*, known as A. Blumenthal, to a duel. Blumenthal did not accept the challenge, however, and soon after Ridge left for San Francisco. In spite of it vicissitudes the paper survived and is still published in Grass Valley. After Ridge's retirement W. S. Byrne left the *National* to join the *Union* and Charles Mitchell came from Auburn and acquired an interest, and then became its sole owner for twenty-seven years.

GREENVILLE: Plumas County.

Bulletin—September 1880. Edited by E. Weed.

HAVILAH: Kern County.

Courier—Weekly, 1866-1869?

Havilah Miner—1872-1874.

HORNITOS: Mariposa County.

Mariposa Democrat—Weekly, June 1856-1857. Published in Mariposa.

HORSETOWN: Shasta County.

Northern Argus—1857-1868. Published by James Hart in 1865.

INDEPENDENCE: Inyo County.

Inyo Independent—July 1870. First paper in the Owens Valley. P. A. Chalfant, James E. Parker, editors. First printed on the old Ames press. Still published. P. A. Chalfant left the *Independent* to start the *Inyo Register* in Bishop in 1885.

Inyo Lancet—1871. Edited by Goodale, Hill and Co. Printed in the office of the *Inyo Independent*, but a political rival.

IONE: Amador County.

Amador Times—See *Ione News.*

Chronicle—Weekly, 1861, for a few months. Published by Folger and Company. When Folger moved to Alpine County it is possible that he took the paper along and merged it with the *Alpine Chronicle*, published in Markleeville.

Ione News—Established by Haley and Company in

1877. It ceased publication in November 1880 because of lack of financial support.

IOWA HILL: Placer County.

Iowa Hill News—Weekly, September 1855-November 1857. Followed by *North San Juan Star* and *Hydraulic Press*. First issue in Iowa Hill in September 15, 1855. J. P. Olmstead and Miller, publishers. Its main editorial objective was the division of Placer County, in which campaign it failed. The paper was moved to North San Juan in November 1857, with Olmstead still publisher and Thomas Waters as partner. The name was changed to the *North San Juan Star*. When it was sold to Benjamin P. Avery tht name was again changed to *Hydraulic Press*. Another change in ownership, to William Baumann, also changed the name, to *San Juan Press*.

Patriot—Weekly, 1859. Established by E. B. Boust of the *Placer Courier*, to replace the *News* that had been removed to North San Juan. In spite of a hard struggle to survive, Boust continued the paper until May 1, 1860, when he too moved on, this time to Dutch Flat, where he started the *Enquirer*.

JACKSON: Amador County.

Amador Dispatch—Weekly, 1858-1880. Published by J. Heckendorn and George Payne. It was first put out at

Lancha Plana (Flat Boat), so-called because of the flat boat ferries which carried gold seekers across the river to the mines. The paper was first printed on an old roller press during the boom days of Lancha Plana; and then was purchased by a man named Mullen, who moved it to Jackson, where it was a Democratic sheet. In 1860 it was sold to George Payne and William Penry, who turned it into an anti-administration paper and it wielded considerable political power. When Lincoln was assassinated the paper was suppressed and its publishers, Penry and Payne, were taken to Alcatraz Island where they were incarcerated because of their political leanings. After a month on the Island they were released and returned to Jackson where they reopened the *Dispatch* office and began to publish, with the same political policies as before. However, public opinion had calmed down and their views were no longer considered a matter for drastic action. L. P. Hall, "Long Primer," who had been associated with the *Auburn Democratic Weekly*, also had an interest in the *Dispatch*. It is told that he could stand up to a *case* and set an editorial without a manuscript, a feat few editors were able to perform.

While the publishers of the *Dispatch* were on Alcatraz Island, R. M. Briggs took over the newspaper office to print the *Union Record*. His editorials were widely read in the East. When the *Dispatch* was revived the *Union Record* ceased.

Amador Ledger & Record—1855-1875-? First issue October 27, 1855. Published first in Volcano as *Weekly Ledger* until 1857, when it became *Amador Weekly Ledger*. 1865, published by T. A. Springer. It was Democratic until the Civil War, when it became Union-Democrat. Springer was a fine printer and later took the job as State Printer for California, at which time Grant Springer took over management of the *Ledger*, with R. M. Briggs and J. A. Eagon handling the editorial policies. In 1875 it was under the management of Richard Webb.

Amador Sentinel—1854-1862. First published by Charles Boynton of the *Owl*, Mokelumne Hill. He carried the issues to Jackson under his arm and distributed them in person, until he secured his own press in Jackson. He sold out to O. D. Avaline in 1857. The paper was published until 1862, when Avaline shut down the press to join the Union Army.

Bell—August-September, 1855. A humorous sheet that ran for only two issues. Printed on *Sentinel* press.

Democratic Standard — Campaign paper of 1856. Edited and published by Homer King. Issued for only three months from the *Sentinel* press.

Independent—August-September 1858. Another political campaign paper edited by J. H. Dennis in behalf of the Independent ticket.

Owl— 1853-1854. A humorous paper published by Charles Boynton, the father of newspapers in Amador County. He ran off several issues of this paper from the type of the *Chronicle*, Mokelumne Hill, with which he was associated. It is said that he frequently swam the river with the edition strapped to his head, and that he never went to Mokelumne Hill without having a fight over his publication.

Prospector—May 1854. Printed by M. B. Clark, A. Badlam, and W. J. Wallace, who were officers of the Ditch Company, and who turned newspaper publishers to kill time. It ran a year and paid its way through advertising.

Sentinel—Second paper of the name. Started in June 1879, by Turner, McNeil and Briggs. Republican in politics and still being published in 1880 by Turner and Sanborn.

Student's Banner—March 30, 1858. One issue, put out by G. O. Ash and N. C. Briggs to aid a school exhibition in Jackson.

Union Record—See *Amador Dispatch*.

KNIGHT'S FERRY: Stanislaus County.

Bee (sometimes called *Ferry Bee*)—1859. Published by W. J. Collier. The paper's makeup was four pages, six columns to a page, and sold for 25c per copy. J. B. Kennedy succeeded Collier after a few issues. The life of the paper was only fourteen months; when it was succeeded by the *Stanislaus Index*.

Stanislaus Index—1861-1862. Harrison and Whicher, publishers. Suspended publication in 1862.

La Porte (Rabbit Creek): Plumas County.

Mountain Messenger—1855. First issue was in the fall of 1855. A. T. Dewey, publisher. In 1859 W. S. Byrne was associated with Dewey. Destroyed by fire in 1861, and in 1862 Dewey bought out Byrne's interest, and the following year J. A. Vaughn became a partner. In 1864 Dewey's relative, E. M. Dewey, purchased an interest. From February 1864 the paper was published in Downieville by Dewey and Vaughan. In 1868 E. M. Dewey sold his interest to E. K. Downer and D. Whitney, but Whitney soon dropped out and the publishers were Downer and Vaughan. See *Gibsonville Herald*.

Lundy: Mono County.

Homer Mining Index—Weekly, 1880-? Considered the best newspaper printed in Mono County, and an excellent source of information on early mining camps of the vicinity. J. W. E. Townsend, editor. Known as "Lyin'

Jim Townsend." Said to have been the original of "Truthful James" of Bret Harte.

MAMMOTH CITY: Mono County.

Mammoth City Herald—Semi-weekly, weekly, 1879-1880? The first paper published in Mammoth City. W. W. Barnes, first publisher, editor, distributor. R. D. Bogart, partner, July to September, 1879.

Mammoth City Times—Weekly, semi-weekly. 1879-1880? Also known as *Lake Mining Review*, a rival of the *Herald*. John Gilson, publisher; R. D. Bogart, editor.

MARIPOSA: Mariposa County.

Chronicle (*Gazette*)—January 20, 1854-March 1855. Owned by W. T. Whitacre and A. S. Gould. Ownership changed the first year to John C. Hopper and C. W. Blaisdell. Purchased in 1855 by L. A. Holmes and the name changed to *Gazette*, with the first issue under the new masthead March 12, 1855. It never missed an issue. The press upon which it was printed was a Washington hand press brought around the Horn to San Francisco and then shipped to Mariposa by Wells Fargo Express. Type was hand set and the subscription price was $5.00 per year. It was a weekly of four pages, giving news in a non-partisan manner. The first description of the Yosemite Valley was printed July 12, 1855 in the *Gazette*, following the trip of J. M. Hutchings into the valley. In 1867 the paper was published by A. M. Sweeney. It is one of the oldest of the continuously published newspapers in California. Still going.

Democrat—Published in Hornitos, June 1856-1858. D. B. Milne and Warren Bear were the original owners. M. Godfrey was the publisher after it moved to Mariposa.

Free Press—1863-1866. J. H. Laurence, publisher in 1865.

Gazette—See *Chronicle*.

Mail—1866-1869. Angevine Reynolds, publisher. He arrived in California in 1849 and settled on Mariposa Creek.

Star—June 1858. J. W. Ross and James Laurence, editors. A Democratic paper.

MARKLEEVILLE: Alpine County.

Alpine Chronicle—See *Bodie Chronicle*, 1865-1867. Published by Robert Folger.

Alpine Signal—Weekly, July 1878-1879.

MEADOW LAKE: Nevada County.

Sun—1866 for a few months. Published by W. Lyon. H. G. Rollin and Judge F. Tilford.

MILLERTON: Fresno County.

Expositor—1870-1874. Became *Fresno Expositor*.

MOKELUMNE HILL: Calaveras County.

Calaveras Chronicle — Weekly. First issue October 9, 1851. This was the second paper published in the southern mines. Owned by H. Hamilton, J. J. Ayres and H. A. DeCourcey, the latter being editor from 1851-1852. He came from the *Nevada Journal*. In 1852 he fought a duel with a man namel Carter, and survived his wounds. From 1852 to 1854 Hamilton conducted the paper, and then it was taken over by George Shuler, who ran it until 1857. with J. M. Bengay and J. O'Meara as editors. In 1857 John Shannon became owner and editor. When James O'Meara left the *Calaveras Chronicle* he hied himself to San Francisco where he became prominent because of his writings on the Broderick-Terry duel and the Second Vigilance Committee. The *Chronicle* office was destroyed by fire during its career in the early 1850s, but this did not deter its progress. It was the only newspaper printed in English in Mokelumne Hill.

Quampeag Coyote — May 1855. A humorous sheet edited under the pseudonyms of Parthenon, Slimface and Peter Noodles.

MONITOR: Alpine County.

Alpine Miner — June 1864-September 1874. S. G. Lewis, publisher.

Gazette—1865. Published by Noble and Company.

MURPHY'S: Calaveras County.

News—Semi-weekly, weekly, 1856. First issue July 21, 1856. Edited by D. Youcham and J. Palache. Lasted but one month.

NEVADA CITY: Nevada County.

Coyote—1854. Issued from the office of the *Journal* by W. A. Potter. One issue only.

Daily Gazette—1864-1874. O. P. Stidger and Company, publishers; O. P. Stidger, editor. Material from the *San Juan Press*. In 1872 the material of the *Grass Valley National* was added. Ceased publication in 1874. Others who edited the paper were William Sear, E. F. Bean and A. Morse.

Daily Transcript—1860-? First daily paper in Nevada County. First issued September 6, 1860. N. P. Brown, James Allen, John P. Skelton, and A. Casamayou. Allen held the editorial post. In 1861 N. P. Brown was editor and owner. In 1862 E. G. Waite purchased an interest and became the editor. In 1877 N. P. Brown and G. A. Baily were the owners, with Brown as editor. Leonard S. Calkins became associated with Brown in 1878 and was the editor. Under Calkins the paper appeared as a daily except Monday, and was a reliable source of news on the mines. It was widely read in the east.

Nevada Democrat—1854-1863. Niles Searls and T. J. Rolfe, first publishers. Tallman Rolfe resumed the editorship in 1863 shortly before the paper ceased publication. (See *Young America.*)

Nevada Journal—1851-1863. First issue in April 1851. Published as the second paper in a California mining town, and the first in the northern mines. Warren B. Ewer was the first editor and publisher. It was next run by Alban and DeCourcey, with the latter as the editor. In 1852, A. A. Sargent was editor, followed by the firm of Sargent and E. R. Budd. In 1854 Budd assumed control. The next year N. P. Brown and Company were publishers, with Sargent as editor. He retired in 1855 and the firm became E. G. Waite, N. P. Brown, John Skelton, H. M. Fuller Company, publishers, with Waite as editor. The firm remained the same until 1856 when Fuller and Skelton retired and Sargent again became editor for about three months. At this time the newspaper office was destroyed by fire. From then until 1858 the firm was Brown and Waite, then it became Lockwood, Thompson and Waite, with Waite as editor. When Waite retired the editor's chair was filled by the Reverend B. Birely. Of these men Ewer was the scholarly journalist who assumed the editorship of the *Mining and Scientific Press.* A. A. Sargent became Senator, and later Minister to Germany. The paper was politically Whig in sentiment to July 1855, when it advocated the principles of the American Party. In 1857-1858 it was a supporter of Douglas.

Miner's Spectacles—Also known as *Muggins Mirror*. A humorous sheet published in the winter of 1855. It was put out on the press of the *Journal* by John Patterson, N. P. Brown and John Skelton. It was short lived.

Miner's Spy Glass—Winter of 1855. Edited by John S. Foster from the *Democrat*. A temperance paper that ran for only two issues.

Tri-Weekly Herald—1878-? Publishers were J. B. Gray, E. A. Davis, H. L. Herzinger. Later it was edited by R. E. Robinson and D. Delim. The paper was devoted to mining news of Nevada County.

Young America—1853-1863. First issue September 14, 1853. R. A. Davidge was the editor. In 1854 Warren B. Ewer became the editor, with Niles Searls, J. H. Boardman and Russell as publishers. The name was changed to the *Nevada Democrat*.

NORTH SAN JUAN: Nevada County.

Hydraulic Press—(See *Iowa Hill News*, *North San Juan Star*, *San Juan Press*.) 1858-1860. Benjamin P. Avery bought out the *North San Juan Star* and changed the name to the *Hydraulic Press*.

OROVILLE DAILY BUTTE RECORD.

VOLUME 2 — OROVILLE, BUTTE COUNTY, CALIFORNIA, THURSDAY, JANUARY 7, 1858. — NUMBER 149.

Butte Record.

THOS. BOYCE, ADVERTISING AGENCY, SAN FRANCISCO. Authorized Agent!

LEGAL NOTICES.

SUMMONS

SUMMONS

NOTICE

NOTICE OF DISSOLUTION

FERRY NOTICE

SAN FRANCISCO ADV'TS.

QURTZ MINING Machinery.

Bradford's Patent Ore Separator.

J. Regan's Steam Refined CANDY MANUFACTORY!

DR. P. M. O'BRIEN, VALLEJO STREET, SAN FRANCISCO

To the Citizens of California.

CAUTION!

Wolfe's Scheidam Aromatic SCHNAPPS,

Perfectly Pure Medical Tonic

WOLFE'S Scheidam Aromatic Schnapps.

BUSINESS CARDS.

Justice of the Peace,

CONSTABLE.

Attorney & Counselor at Law. NOTARY PUBLIC.

CONSTABLE. Collector and Real Estate Agent.

JAMES O'BRIEN, M. D.

GEO. D. FRENCH, County Surveyor.

EDWARD DONOHUE. Justice of the Peace,

KLEINE & GASTON Attorneys & Counselors at Law.

Notary Public,

BUNT & RHODES Attorneys & Counselors at Law, Oroville.

CHARLES F. LOTT, Attorney & Counselor at Law, AND NOTARY PUBLIC. OROVILLE, BUTTE COUNTY.

GRANGER & CHEESMAN, ATTORNEYS & COUNSELLORS AT LAW.

BURLINGAME & MORSE DENTISTS,

DR. MYERS, DENTIST.

THOMAS WELLS. ATTORNEY AT LAW, OROVILLE, BUTTE COUNTY.

GEORGE E. SMITH, Watchmaker & Jeweler, OROVILLE

RIPE BOTTLED London Porter! 150

WANTED. 10,000, Sash, Doors and Blinds!

MISCELLANEOUS.

POST OFFICE Literary Depot!

BOOKS,

Standard Works.

School Books.

Stationery.

Cutlery,

Christmas Presents.

OPPOSITION LINE! CHEAP JOHN, AUCTION AND COMMISSION MERCHANT!

TOBACCO AND CIGARS

Redington & Co. Wholesale Druggists, 107 Clay St., San Francisco,

Lost--$10 Reward!

Fresh Butter! Petaluma Butter

Oroville Hay Scales.

HOTELS, SALOONS, &C.

ST. NICHOLAS HOTEL, AND General Stage Office, OROVILLE. FRANK JOHNSON........Proprietor.

The Table

The Beds

The Bar

HAUN HOUSE. Marysville.

MERCHANTS HOTEL. MARYSVILLE

National Hotel! BIDWELL.

MISCELLANEOUS.

ALTA EXPRESS CO. Daily Expresses! SAN FRANCISCO.

BANK EXCHANGE BAR AND BILLIARD SALOON.

THE BAR

The Billiard Tables

OROVILLE DAILY BUTTE RECORD, published from Oroville.

THE SAN JUAN PRESS.

The Truth—Onward and Upward—God Defend the Right.

Vol. 1. NORTH SAN JUAN, NEVADA COUNTY, SATURDAY, FEBRUARY 6, 1864. No. 37—New Series.

THE SAN JUAN PRESS.

ISSUED EVERY SUNDAY MORNING.

O. P. STIDGER,

Terms for the Paper.

Terms for Advertising.

Societies.

Hose Companies.

Professional Cards.

A Card.

JOHN STOTLAR, M. D.,
PHYSICIAN AND SURGEON,

DR. STOTLAR—for more than twenty-six years a practitioner in Medicine and Surgery, and for the last four years a resident of North San Juan—respectfully returns thanks to his old friends for their past patronage, and takes this occasion to say that he continues the practice of Medicine and Surgery, in all its branches, and is prepared to attend to all calls in the line of his profession.

Obstetrics, and diseases incident to women and children, particularly attended to.

MEDICATED BATHS,
for the cure of all kinds of disease, furnished to patients.

Office and Baths, on the north side of Main street, one door east of Frank Smith's store.

Medical Notice.

JAMES SIMPSON, M. D.,

RESPECTFULLY informs the people of Bridgeport township, and the public generally, that he has located permanently at North San Juan, in the practice of

MEDICINE AND SURGERY

He can be consulted at all hours of the day—when not professionally absent—at his office, in O. P. Stidger's Law office, Main street.

Residence at the extreme west end of San Francisco street, north side. julal-tf

J. B. JOHNSON,
ATTORNEY AT LAW, NOTARY PUBLIC,
Commissioner of Deeds
FOR NEVADA TERRITORY,
And Township Clerk.

OFFICE on Main street, North San Juan one door east of Frank Smith's Hardware store, where he will promptly attend to any business in the line of his profession.

O. P. STIDGER,
Attorney at Law,
NOTARY PUBLIC, AND CONVEYANCER,
AND
COMMISSIONER OF DEEDS,
For Nevada Territory.

OFFICE in the brick building, north side of Main street, North San Juan, west of and adjoining E. V. Hatfield's store.

D. R. SAMPLE,
Attorney and Counsellor at Law,
Office corner 3d and D streets,
Marysville.

C. G. HUBBARD,
Attorney and Counsellor at Law,
Office corner Third and D streets,
Marysville, Cal.

HATCH & McQUAID,
Attorneys at Law,
Marysville, Cal.

DENTISTRY.

P. BOLTON, D. D. S.,

Artificial Teeth

SPECIMENS OF GOLD BEARING QUARTZ.

BOOT AND SHOE MAKING.

REPAIRING done in good style, and with dispatch.

A continuance of patronage is respectfully solicited. N. B. WHITTIER.

WATCHES, CLOCKS, and Jewelry.

A GOOD assortment kept constantly on hand, and for sale cheap. Call and see.

All kinds of Watches, Clocks and Jewelry repaired in the best possible manner, and warranted.

Jewelry made to order.

Main street, North San Juan, Opposite Block & Furth's.

Painting.

JAMES C. CARPENTER is prepared to perform all kinds of

Plain and Fancy Painting.

House and sign painting and Graining neatly executed.

Shop on south side of Main street, opposite High street, North San Juan.

Tailoring.

COATS, PANTS, VESTS, &c., of the latest styles, manufactured to order, of the best materials. Mending of all kinds of garments neatly executed by the undersigned, at his shop on the south side of Main street, four doors west of the San Juan Exchange.

BEN. WOOD.

SQUARE UP!

J. W. GUTHRIE & BRO.

BEEF,
MUTTON,
PORK,
VEAL,
SAUSAGES,
LARD, &c.

S. W. GUTHRIE.

SCHWARTZ & CO.

153 Third street,

Importers and Wholesale Dealers in

Sheet-Iron & Copper Ware,

HARDWARE, STOVES, TIN,
CROCKERY, GLASSWARE, PUMPS,
Kitchen Furniture, &c.

Dealers in Cots, Cribs, Spring Mattresses, and every description of office, household and store furniture.

Second-hand Furniture bought and sold.

Furniture repaired with neatness and dispatch.

Marysville, June 15, 1863.

GARDEN SEEDS!

IMPORTED direct from the well known seedmen, J. M. Thorburn, & Co., New York, by

GEORGE D. DORNIN,
Express Building, North San Juan.

Farmers and gardeners may rely upon finding at this establishment

FRESH AND PURE SEEDS,

at prices as favorable as any in the State.

Dealers supplied in quantities to suit.

San Juan Press, showing O. P. Stidger as editor and publisher.

Independent—Weekly, April 1878-April 1880. A. O. Porter, J. R. Robinson. publishers. A paper devoted exclusively to home interests.

North San Juan Press—The property of the *Hydraulic Press*. The paper was purchased by O. P. Stidger, who continued the publication under the same name until March of 1864, when it was moved to Nevada City and became the *Nevada City Daily Gazette*.

North San Juan Star — 1857-1858. Edited by J. P. Olmstead and Thomas Waters. Sold in 1858 to become the *Hydraulic Press*.

North San Juan Times—Weekly, 1873-1878.

War Club—Semi-weekly, 1872.

OROVILLE: Butte County.

Butte Democrat—August 1857-?

Butte Record — See Bidwell's Bar *Weekly Butte Record*.

Mercury — 1877. Name changed to *Daily Mercury* in 1883.

North Californian—November 1855-April 1857. Followed in 1858 by the *Morning Advertiser*. Published by C. G. Lincoln and Company.

Register—Weekly, 1877. Published by Biggs in 1879.

Weekly Union—1862-1864. Merged with *Weekly Butte Record* as *Oroville Union Record.* Published by S. G. Lewis in 1867. Later *Chico Record.*

PANAMINT: Inyo County.

News—1874-1875. Published tri-weekly by Panamint Publishing Company. T. S. Harris and D. P. Carr, editors. Moved to Darwin, 1875. See *Coso Mining News.*

PLACERVILLE: El Dorado County.

American—Weekly, July 1855-November 1859. Edited by Wadsworth and Childs from July 1855 to August 1856. Then Harvey and Childs, to November 1857. Then Barstow Park, with Cole and Dietz, editors. Failed in 1859.

Appeal—March to May 1853. A Democratic paper published by W. S. Fleming and Company.

Argus—Tri-weekly, 1857-February 1860. See *Empire County Argus,* Coloma. First issue August 13, 1857; Captain Frank Stewart, editor. Succeeded by tri-weekly *Register,* semi-weekly *Register,* semi-weekly *Observer,* February 2, 1859, with O. L. C. and J. D. Fairchild as publishers and Captain Stewart as editor. Discontinued February 4, 1860.

Central Californian—Semi-weekly, August 1860-? Hon. J. G. McCallum, publisher. A campaign weekly paper for Douglas and Johnson. Richard Cole, editor, followed Jan. 1, 1861, by O. D. Avaline.

Coloma Times—March 1860-October 1861. George O. Kies and S. B. Weller, publishers. Became *Placerville Times*, November 3, 1861, with Kies as publisher.

Courier—Weekly, June 1866-1867. Lyers and Yarnell, publishers.

El Dorado County Journal—Weekly, January 1856. See *Miner's Advocate* of Diamond Springs.

El Dorado County Union—Weekly, June 28, 1861-July 20, 1861. Richard Cole, editor. Ceased publication after becoming a daily.

El Dorado News—December 1851-May 1853. See *El Dorado News*, Coloma.

El Dorado Republican—Second paper to be issued by that name. Published for the political campaign of 1857.

Herald—April-November, 1853. F. A. Bee and W. Wadsworth, publishers. A Democratic campaign paper.

Mirror—Weekly, 1865-1866.

Mountain Democrat—Weekly, 1854-? Appeared first on February 25, 1854. Edited by D. W. Gelwicks and William January. Published continuously except for a fire in 1856. On August 22, 1860 it became the semi-weekly *Mountain Democrat* with George P. Johnson taking the place of January, who was elected clerk of El Dorado County in 1859. Returned to weekly publication in 1861.

In January of 1867 George O. Kies and T. J. Caystile became owners and editors. December 20, 1872, W. A. Selkirk bought a controlling interest with Kies as partner until 1874, when Selkirk became sole owner. In 1860 Selkirk and E. A. Smith; 1881 Selkirk bought out Smith. In November 1862 General Wright, commander of the Department of the Pacific forbade the sending of the paper through the mail or expresses because of its political affiliations. See *El Dorado Republican.*

News — Weekly, started by Fumarton and Yarnell. Printed on the press of the *Union.* First issue August 14, 1861. Probably the same as the *Placerville News,* published by D. J. and H. A. Yarnell.

Observer—Semi-weekly. Editors, O. L. C. and J. D. Fairchild. First issued on February 2, 1859. Discontinued in 1860. Printed on the *Argus* press.

Recorder—1865-1866.

Republican—August 7, 1861, first issue. D. deGolia, publisher; Bowman, editor; succeeded by Thomas Fitch. Discontinued in 1862. Revived in 1863 by B. F. Davis. It was still being published in 1880.

QUINCY: Plumas County.

Fillmore Banner—Campaign paper of 1856. Edited by Silas Caulkins and printed on the press of the *Old Mountaineer.*

Old Mountaineer—1855-July 1857. First newspaper in Plumas County. First edition August 1855. Edited and published by John K. Lovejoy and Edward McElwain. Sold to John Lewis and James McNabb in 1857. The name was then changed to the *Plumas Argus*. During the political campaign of 1856 three columns of the paper were edited by Dr. A. Fredonyer, an ardent Republican, who carried on a lively editorial debate with the gentlemen of the *Plumas Democrat* and the *Fillmore Banner*.

Plumas Argus—July 1857. Taken over by the *Old Mountaineer*. Published until 1860, when it was taken over by the sheriff. It was revived the same year and published for four months by John Lewis and Edward McElwain. The press was then moved to Carson City, Nevada, where the name was changed to the *Silver Age*.

Plumas Democrat—Campaign paper of 1856, edited by John S. Ward and E. T. Hogan. This paper was printed upon the press of the *Old Mountaineer*.

Plumas National—1866-? Edited by H. L. Gear until 1869 when L. C. Charles and William E. Ward took over the paper. Charles sold his interest in 1871 to Ward. The paper was still published in 1880.

Plumas Standard—Weekly, 1859-1863. Thomas Bail and Lewis Curtz, editors in 1859. Matthew Lynch took over in 1860, and three years later moved the paper to Downieville. See *Downieville Standard*.

Prospector—Edited and published by Alexander Badlam, who afterwards became the assessor of San Francisco County.

Quincy Union—1862-1869. A Union Party paper published by Leonard and Powers. The Plumas Printing Company, with John Buckbee as editor, took over the paper in 1864. W. W. Kellogg, who had come to Plumas County in 1858, became the editor and publisher soon afterward, and he held the post for some eight years. He then entered politics and was elected to the State Legislature on the Republican ticket. He had, however, gone to La Porte in 1868 when the paper was moved there, and in 1869 the plant was destroyed by fire and suffered such losses that publication ceased.

SAN ANDREAS: Calaveras County.

Calaveras Advertiser—Weekly, 1869-1881.

Calaveras Citizen—1871-? C. R. Beal, editor and publisher. Name changed to *Calaveras Prospect and Citizen.*

Calaveras Times—May-June, 1863.

Calaveras Union — October 11, 1856 - November 8, 1857. A. C. Lewis, editor and publisher. A campaign paper in 1864. W. W. Kellogg, who had come to Plumas County in 1858, became the editor and publisher soon Company, with John Buckbee as editor, took over the paper in favor of the American Party.

Foothill Democrat—Weekly, 1874-?

Mountain News—Weekly, 1867-1868. J. D. Spencer, editor and publisher.

San Andreas Independent — 1856-1860. Paper published at Stockton as the *Morning Independent*. B. P. Kooser, editor.

San Andreas Register—Weekly, 1863-1868. Published in 1867 by Ransom, Benham and Denig.

SHASTA: Shasta County.

Courier — Weekly, 1852. First issue March 12. Founded by A. Skillman and J. C. Hinckley; Samuel Dosh, editor. The first paper published north of Marysville. It was begun as an independent in politics, but became Democratic in sentiment in 1855. As was the fate of so many newspaper offices it was destroyed by fire in the first year of life, and suspended for four months. In June 1853 it again suffered loss by fire, but this time the press was saved and the *Courier* continued to print, even though the issues were on half-sheets. In 1858 Skillman and Dosh became the sole owners.

Herald—James R. Keene, editor. See *Republican*.

Republican — October 10, 1855-1861. Favored the American Party. J. C. Hinckley, who had been with the *Courier*, and Gillette, were first owners and editors, until May 1859. It was then published by J. R. Keene and then was taken over by Street and Moffatt. The paper was supported by adherents of the LeCompton Policy in regard to the Kansas question. It also supported President Buchanan. Suspended in 1861, under the name of *Shasta Herald.*

Vigilante — June 1856-? G. K. Godfrey, editor. It lasted but one month and was printed to support the reforms of the vigilante movement.

SILVER MOUNTAIN: Alpine County.

Alpine Chronicle—See *Bodie Chronicle.*

Bulletin—1865. Published by D. S. Lane, and W. O. Hayes, in 1867.

Silver Mountain Miner—Weekly, April-June 1868.

SONORA: Tuolumne County.

American Eagle—Weekly, May-August 1864. George L. Sharrats, publisher.

American Flag — Weekly, 1861-1864. First issue on November 1, 1861. Strictly a Union paper. H. B. McNeil, Oliver Wolcott, Seth Sneden, editors, and D. O. McCarthy, a livery stable owner, was the publisher. During the great storm of 1862 the paper was published on half-sheets. Suspended publication in February 1862. A charge of murder was brought against the publisher, probably by the secessionists, and he was thrown in jail on the hope that the paper would cease to publish. During the Civil War McCarthy moved the paper to San Francisco.

Democratic Age—Weekly, 1860.

Mountain Whig—Weekly for five weeks in summer of 1852. The only Whig party paper in the southern mines. Published by J. W. Dunn.

Sonora Herald—Weekly, 1850-1859. Resumed, 1865-1867. The first issue of the *Herald* was distributed on July 4, 1850, its editors John White and John G. Marvin. It was the first newspaper printed in a California mining town. The first issues were printed on 9″x13″ foolscap and sold for fifty cent a copy. The twelfth issue saw it enlarged to 12″x17″. It was printed on wrapping paper, as no newsprint was available. The first printer was Enos Christman, who learned his trade in Pennsylvania and came to California via the Horn, arriving in San Francisco February 12, 1850. By early summer he had gone to Sonora and the following from his diary tells of his printing the first issue of the *Herald:* "On Wednesday afternoon July 3, after having worked off the first edition of the *Herald* in the *Times* office at Stockton, the proprietor solicited me to take a horse and start immediately for Sonora . . . in order that the paper might be distributed. . . . The day after my arrival I distributed the copies of the first number throughout the town."

The paper was printed on an old Ramage press which

was brought around the Horn to California in 1834 on order of Augustin V. Zamorano, California's first printer. The press was built in Philadelphia, and was sold to Zamorano from Boston by Thomas Shaw. The price was $460 American dollars. The platen and frame of the press were of wood. The bed for the forms, of stone, and the screw used for the impression, iron. The old Ramage that was first used to print *manifestos* for the Mexican government, went from Monterey to San Francisco, to Sacramento, back to San Francisco and then to Stockton, where it served the first printer in Stockton. It was sold by him to Marvin and White of Sonora in the summer of 1850. By 1851 the press was too small to print the larger sized *Herald*, and it was sold to Gore of Columbia, publisher of the *Star*. The sticks for composing were those that had been whittled by Enos Christman from a pine plank.

Upon the twelfth issue of the *Herald*, White transferred his interest to J. R. Reynolds, who held it for only two weeks and sold to T. Haley, who, in turn sold to Dr. Lewis C. Gunn. The 15th, 16th and 17th issues were published under the joint ownership of Marvin and Gunn; and the 18th issue carried the name of Enos Christman in the place of Judge Marvin. To the 40th issue Christman was associated with the paper and then Gunn took over sole ownership until May 1852, when Walter Murray and James O'Sullivan assumed ownership. February 19, 1853,

O'Sullivan sold his interest to Murray, who, in turn, sold back to Gunn. About this time James Coffroth became an employee of the *Herald*. From April 1854, O'Sullivan and Alexander Murray, brother of Walter, became proprietors and the paper continued to see-saw in ownership until 1856. In July that year it became the *Daily Sonora Herald*, and was independent in its political views. This newspaper was the first in California to advocate title in fee simple for mineral bearing land.

Tuolumne Courier—1857-1866. Published in Columbia.

Tuolumne Independent—1872-1876. John C. and William A. Duchow, editors.

Union Democrat—Weekly, 1854-1856? First issue July 1, 1854. It was the only paper wth Democratic sentiments in Sonora. It was published by A. N. Francisco. In 1855 the editor was C. Donovan. In 1856 Otis Greenwood was editor and Francisco publisher. Prentice Mulford was a writer for it in 1871, under the title of "Dogberry." In 1869 William A. Arthur was editor, but died in October of that year. In 1875 W. H. Roberts and E. H. Clugh were the owners.

SUTTER CREEK: Amador County.

Foothills Ensign—1875. Devoted to the advancement of the County of Amador. "Fearless and Independent in everything, neutral in nothing." It was published every Friday.

Independent—1873-1874. A daily paper published by R. V. Chadd. It was popular for a short time because of its devotion to local items. It died, however, from lack of subscribers. The materials were purchased by Richard Webb of the *Ione Ledger*.

TUOLUMNE: Tuolumne County.

News—Weekly, 1868-1869. First issue February 14, 1868. J. D. Spencer, editor and publisher. Issued from the upper floor of the Ross House every Friday. A Democratic organ and responsible for the breaking up of the Land Office ring in Stockton. It also advocated the "no fence" law. The last issue of the paper in Tuolumne City was November 29, 1861. The paper ceased issue when its editor and publisher decided that the coming of the railroad had killed the chances of Tuolumne City, and he moved to Modesto.

VOLCANO: Amador County.

Ledger — Weekly, October 27, 1857. Thomas A. Springer, E. A. Dangerfield, editors and publishers. Moved to Jackson in April 1858.

WEAVERVILLE: Trinity County.

Democrat—1855-1856. Edited by H. J. Howe and J. Crawford.

Journal—First issue January 26, 1856. Took over the *Times*. It is now one of the oldest papers in California, and has never missed an issue.

Times—December 1854. First published by Rowe and Conway. Taken over by *Journal*.

Trinity Press—1870-1871.

Trinity Journal—See *Journal*.

YANKEE JIM'S: Placer County.

Mountain Courier—December 1856-March 1857. Published during the winter of 1857. Parker and Graves, publishers. Office was attached for debt and the paper died.

Placer Courier—July 4, 1857-1863. First issue July 4, 1857. E. B. Boust, editor. It used the materials left over from the *Mountain Courier*. The paper was purchased by R. J. Steele in November 1858, and moved to Forest Hill the following spring. It was published by Steele until December 1860 when it was sold to Philip Lynch, who continued it until 1863.

YREKA: Siskiyou County.

Chronicle—1856-1859. Started by J. W. A'Neal after he withdrew from the *Union*. His partner was W. P. Fair, husband of the notorious Laura Fair who shot A. P. Crittenden on a San Francisco bound ferry boat. Prior to him his brother, S. P. Fair, was editor, in company with Jonas Brown and J. W. A'Neal. W. I. Mayfield and H. S. Stipp were the next publishers, followed by J. A. Glasscock and C. N. Thornbury. In 1859 Mayfield took over the paper with J. W. Oliver as editor. Ceased publication September 1859

Journal—Semi-weekly, also known as *Yreka Journal* and *Northern Journal.* It appeared as an Independent paper in July 1861, succeeding the *Weekly Journal*, with Robert Nixon as publisher. It was a Republican paper and one of the pioneers to sponsor that political party. It became the leading Northern California publication and after the election of 1861 it became a weekly. In 1862-1863 it was a rival of the *Union.*

Northern Journal—1859-1860. J. Dumont, publisher; James M. Bassett, editor. Taken over by *Weekly Journal.*

Weekly Journal—W. I. Mayfield, Joshua Tricle and J. R. Murray, publishers.

Mountain Herald—1853-1855. First edition June 11, 1853. Owners, C. N. Thornbury, W. D. Slade, S. F. Van Choate. Published under the name of Thornbury and Company. The money for the press was raised by citizens of Yreka. An old hand press was brought across the mountains via mule express at a cost of fifty cents per pound.

Van Choate soon retired from partnership and a larger press was needed as the paper rapidly increased its circulation. The paper was an independent in politics and prospered until the American Party became a threat in 1855. The paper was then sold to J. Lytle Cummins, who acted as the representative of Mr. A'Neal, H. G. Ferris, D. D. Colton and J. Tyson. The paper's name was changed to the *Union.*

Union — Outgrowth of the *Mountain Herald.* A. A'Neal, one of the purchaser owners, severed his connection when it became Democratic. He even began a law suit to kill the change in politics, but the jury "hung" and he never renewed his suit. Under the direction of Tyson and Company the paper flourished. The editors were George Freaner, J. D. Turner and Calvin McDonald. In 1858 H. H. Brown and J. Tyson were editors. In 1859 it was published as a tri-weekly, with George Price as editor. H. K. White and Robert Tilden took over, and were followed by A. J. Starling as publisher in 1860. From 1861-1864 White, and later, for short periods, William Page, George Hackett and M. D. Houck were associated with it. In 1867 it was published by William Irvin, and 1878 by John Bird.

GRASS VALLEY TELEGRAPH.

EXTRA.

GRASS VALLEY TELEGRAPH, the extra issued after the fire that destroyed Grass Valley in September, 1854.

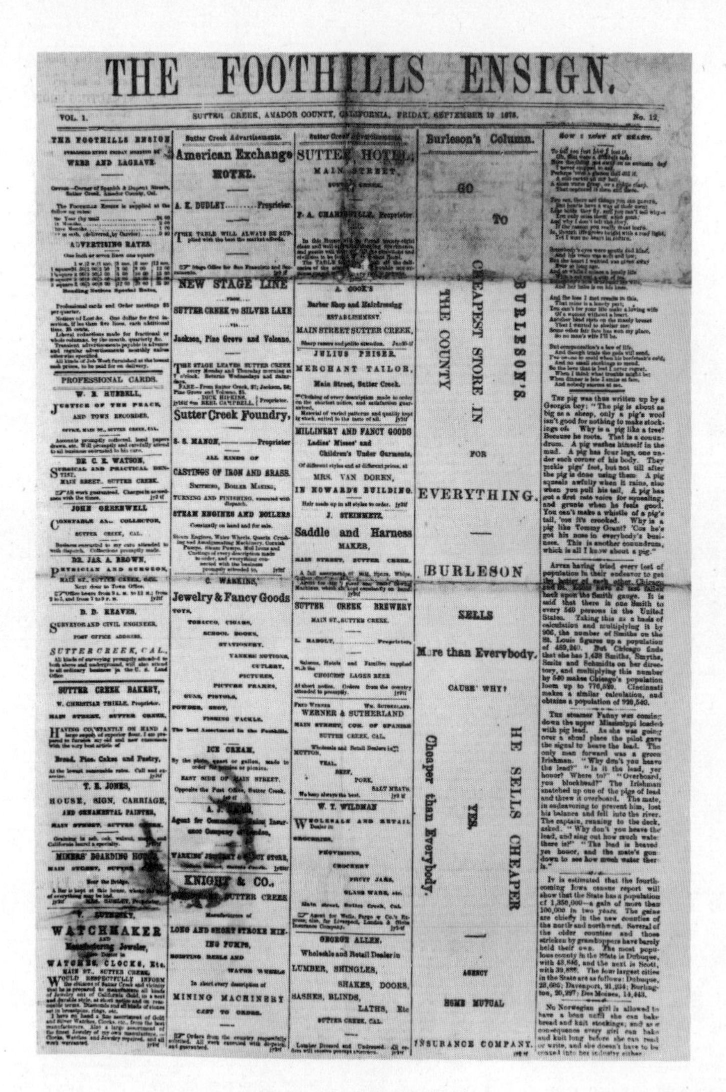

THE FOOTHILLS ENSIGN.

VOL. 1. SUTTER CREEK, AMADOR COUNTY, CALIFORNIA, FRIDAY, SEPTEMBER 10 1875. No. 12.

THE FOOTHILLS ENSIGN

PUBLISHED EVERY FRIDAY MORNING BY WEBB AND LAGRAVE.

ADVERTISING RATES.

PROFESSIONAL CARDS.

W. B. RUSSELL, JUSTICE OF THE PEACE, AND TOWN RECORDER.

DR. C. E. WATSON, SURGICAL AND PRACTICAL DENTIST. MAIN STREET, SUTTER CREEK.

JOHN GREENWELL, CONSTABLE AND COLLECTOR, SUTTER CREEK, CAL.

DR. JAS. A. BROWN, PHYSICIAN AND SURGEON, MAIN ST., SUTTER CREEK, CAL.

D. B. REAVES, SURVEYOR AND CIVIL ENGINEER, SUTTER CREEK, CAL.

SUTTER CREEK BAKERY, W. CHRISTIAN THIELE, Proprietor. MAIN STREET, SUTTER CREEK. Bread, Pies, Cakes and Pastry.

T. B. JONES, HOUSE, SIGN, CARRIAGE, AND ORNAMENTAL PAINTER, MAIN STREET, SUTTER CREEK.

MINERS' BOARDING HOUSE, MAIN STREET, SUTTER CREEK.

WATCHMAKER AND Manufacturing Jeweler, WATCHES, CLOCKS, Etc. MAIN ST., SUTTER CREEK.

Sutter Creek Advertisements.

American Exchange HOTEL. A. K. DUDLEY, Proprietor. THE TABLE WILL ALWAYS BE SUPPLIED WITH THE BEST THE MARKET AFFORDS.

NEW STAGE LINE FROM SUTTER CREEK TO SILVER LAKE VIA Jackson, Pine Grove and Volcano.

Sutter Creek Foundry, S. S. MANON, Proprietor. ALL KINDS OF CASTINGS OF IRON AND BRASS. STEAM ENGINES AND BOILERS.

G. WARKINS, Jewelry & Fancy Goods, TOYS, TOBACCO, CIGARS, SCHOOL BOOKS, STATIONERY, YANKEE NOTIONS, CUTLERY, PICTURES, PICTURE FRAMES, GUNS, PISTOLS, POWDER, SHOT, FISHING TACKLE. The best Assortment in the Foothills. ICE CREAM.

KNIGHT & CO., SUTTER CREEK. LONG AND SHORT STROKE MINING PUMPS, HOISTING REELS AND WATER WHEELS. MINING MACHINERY CAST TO ORDER.

SUTTER HOTEL, MAIN STREET, SUTTER CREEK. P. A. CHARPENTILLE, Proprietor.

A. COOK'S Barber Shop and Hairdressing ESTABLISHMENT. MAIN STREET SUTTER CREEK.

JULIUS PREISER, MERCHANT TAILOR, Main Street, Sutter Creek.

MILLINERY AND FANCY GOODS, Ladies' Misses' and Children's Under Garments. MRS. VAN DOREN, IN HOWARD'S BUILDING.

J. STEINMETZ, Saddle and Harness MAKER, MAIN STREET, SUTTER CREEK.

SUTTER CREEK BREWERY, MAIN ST., SUTTER CREEK. CHOICEST LAGER BEER.

WERNER & SUTHERLAND, MAIN STREET, COR. OF SPANISH, SUTTER CREEK, CAL. MUTTON, VEAL, BEEF, PORK, SALT MEATS.

W. T. WILDMAN, WHOLESALE AND RETAIL Dealer in GROCERIES, PROVISIONS, CROCKERY, FRUIT JARS, GLASS WARE, etc. Main Street, Sutter Creek, Cal.

GEORGE ALLEN, Wholesale and Retail Dealer in LUMBER, SHINGLES, SHAKES, DOORS, SASHES, BLINDS, LATHS, Etc. SUTTER CREEK, CAL.

Burleson's Column.

GO TO BURLESON'S CHEAPEST STORE IN THE COUNTY FOR EVERYTHING.

BURLESON SELLS More than Everybody.

CAUSE' WHY? HE SELLS CHEAPER YES. Cheaper than Everybody.

AGENT HOME MUTUAL INSURANCE COMPANY.

The pig was thus written up by a Georgia boy: "The pig is about as big as a sheep, only a pig's wool isn't good for nothing to make stockings of. Why is a pig like a tree? Because he roots. That is a conundrum. A pig washes himself in the mud. A pig has four legs, one under each corner of his body. They pickle pigs' feet, but not till after the pig is done using them. A pig squeals awfully when it rains, also when you pull his tail. A pig has got a first rate voice for squealing, and grunts when he feels good. You can't make a whistle of a pig's tail, 'cos it's crooked. Why is a pig like Tommy Grant? 'Cos he's got his nose in everybody's business. This is another conundrum, which is all I know about a pig."

After having tried every test of population in their endeavor to get the better of each other, Chicago and St. Louis have at last fallen back upon the Smith gauge. It is said that there is one Smith to every 540 persons in the United States. Taking this as a basis of calculation and multiplying it by 906, the number of Smiths on the St. Louis figures up a population of 489,240. But Chicago finds that she has 1,438 Smiths, Smythe, Smits and Schmidts on her directory, and multiplying this number by 540 makes Chicago's population loom up to 776,520. Cincinnati makes a similar calculation, and obtains a population of 920,540.

The steamer Fanny was coming down the upper Mississippi loaded with pig lead. As she was going over a shoal place the pilot gave the signal to heave the lead. The only man forward was a green Irishman. "Why don't you heave the lead?" "Is it the lead, yer honor? Where to?" "Overboard, you blockhead!" The Irishman snatched up one of the pigs of lead and threw it overboard. The mate, in endeavoring to prevent him, lost his balance and fell into the river. The captain, running to the deck, asked, "Why don't you heave the lead, and sing out how much water there is?" "The lead is heaved yer honor, and the mate's gone down to see how much water there is."

It is estimated that the forthcoming Iowa census report will show that the State has a population of 1,350,000—a gain of more than 100,000 in two years. The gains are chiefly in the new counties of the north and northwest. Several of the older counties and those stricken by grasshoppers have barely held their own. The most populous county in the State is Dubuque, with 43,846, and the next is Scott, with 39,898. The four largest cities in the State are as follows: Dubuque, 28,005; Davenport, 21,234; Burlington, 20,297; Des Moines, 14,443.

No Norwegian girl is allowed to have a beau until she can bake bread and knit stockings; and as a con-sequence every girl can bake and knit long before she can read or write, and she doesn't have to be coaxed into her industry either.

FOOTHILLS ENSIGN

The Newspapers

Alphabetical List of Mining Town Newspapers

Alpine Chronicle, Markleeville — See *Bridgeport Union* and *Bodie Chronicle.*

Alpine Miner, Monitor.

Alpine Signal, Markleeville.

Amador Dispatch, Jackson.

Amador Ledger, Jackson—See *Volcano Weekly Ledger*,

American Eagle, Sonora.

American Flag and *Daily American Flag*, Sonora, San Francisco.

Argus, Tri-Weekly, Placerville — See *Empire County Argus.*

Auburn Herald, Auburn.

Bee, Knights Ferry.

Bell, Jackson.

Bentonian, Benton.

Big Tree Bulletin and *Murphy's Advertiser*, Calaveras Big Tree Grove.

Bodie Chronicle, Bodie — See *Alpine Chronicle*, *Bridgeport Union* and *Bridgeport Chronicle Union.*

Bugle, Downieville.

Bulletin, Silver Mountain.

Butte Democrat, Oroville.

Butte Record, Bidwell's Bar, Oroville.

Calaveras Advertiser, San Andreas.

Calaveras Chronicle, Mokelumne Hill.

Calaveras Citizen, also *Calaveras Prospect and Citizen*, San Andreas.

Calaveras Independent, San Andreas.

Calaveras Mountaineer, Angel's Camp.

Calaveras Times, San Andreas.

Calaveras Union, San Andreas.

California Mountain Messenger, La Porte—See *Mountain Messenger and Gibsonville Herald*, *Gibsonville Trumpet.*

California Staats Zeitung, Mokelumne Hill.

Central Californian, Placerville.

Chronicle, Bridgeport—See *Bodie Chronicle.*

Chronicle, Markleeville—Ione.

Chronicle-Union, Bridgeport.

Citizen, Columbia.

Coloma Times, Placerville, Coloma.

Columbia Clipper, Columbia—See *Columbia Gazette.*

Columbia Gazette, Columbia, merged with *Gazette* and *Southern Mines Advertiser.*

Columbia News, Columbia.

Columbia Star, Columbia.

Columbia Times, Columbia.

Columbian, Columbia.

Coso Mining News, Darwin.

Courier, Copperopolis.

Courier, Havilah.

Courier, Shasta.

Coyote, Nevada City.

Daily Bodie Standard, Bodie—See *Standard News.*

Daily National Gazette, Nevada City—See *Nevada Daily Gazette, North San Juan Times.*

Daily Transcript, Nevada City.

Daily Union, Grass Valley.

Democrat, Downieville.

Democratic Age, Sonora.

Democratic Signal, Auburn.

Democratic Standard, Jackson.

Downieville Standard, Downieville — See *Downieville Weekly Standard.*

Echo, Downieville.

El Dorado County Journal, Diamond Springs.

El Dorado County Union, Placerville.

El Dorado News, Coloma, Placerville.

El Dorado County Republican, Placerville — See *Mountain Democrat.*

El Dorado Republican, Placerville—Second paper under that name.

Empire County Argus, Coloma—See *Tri-Weekly Argus*, *Tri-Weekly Index*, *Tri-Weekly Register*, *Semi-Weekly Observer*, published in Placerville.

Enquirer, Dutch Flat.

Fillmore Banner, Quincy.

Foothill Democrat, San Andreas.

Foothills Ensign, Sutter Creek.

Foothill Weekly, Grass Valley.

Forum, Dutch Flat—See *Placer Times.*

Free Press, Bodie.

Gazette, Georgetown.

Gazette, Monitor.

Gazette, Nevada City.

Gem, Georgetown.

Georgetown Weekly News, Georgetown, merged with *Sierra Democrat*, Forest City.

Gibsonville Herald, Gibsonville, with supplement called *St. Louis News*—See *Mountain Messenger*, La Porte.

Gibsonville Trumpet, Gibsonville—See *Mountain Messenger*, La Porte.

Granite Journal, Granite and Folsom.

Grass Valley Telegraph, Grass Valley—See *National Weekly.*

Grass Valley National Weekly, Grass Valley—See *Daily National Gazette*, Nevada City.

Grass Valley Morning Union, Grass Valley.

Grass Valley Republican, Grass Valley—Became *Truckee Republican.*

Greenville Bulletin, Greenville.

Havilah Miner, Havilah.

Homer Mining Index, Lundy.

Hydraulic Press, North San Juan—See *Iowa Hill News* and *San Juan Press.*

Independent, Jackson.

Independent, North San Juan.

Inyo Independent, Independence.

Inyo Lancet, Independence.

Ione News, Ione.

Iowa Hill News, Iowa Hill—See *North San Juan Star, Hydraulic Press, San Juan Press.*

Iowa Hill Patriot, Iowa Hill.

Journal, Weaverville—Took over the *Times.*

Journal, Yreka.

Mammoth City Herald, Mammoth City.

Mammoth City Times, Mammoth City.

Mariposa Chronicle, Mariposa—See *Mariposa Gazette.*

Mariposa Democrat, Hornitos and Mariposa.

Mariposa Free Press, Mariposa.

Mariposa Gazette—See *Chronicle.*

Mariposa Mail, Mariposa.

Mariposa Star, Mariposa.

Miner's Advocate. Coloma, Diamond Springs, Folsom—See *El Dorado County Journal.*

Miner's Spectacles, Nevada City—Also known as *Muggins Mirror.*

Miner's Spy Glass, Nevada City.

Mining Journal, Grass Valley.

Morning News, Bodie—See *Standard News.*

Morning Transcript, Nevada City.

Morning Union, Grass Valley—Titles vary.

Mountain Courier, Yankee Jim's.

Mountain Democrat, Placerville — See *El Dorado Republican.*

Mountain Echo, Angels Camp.

Mountain Echo, Downieville—Became *Sierra Citizen.*

Mountain Herald, Yreka—See *Yreka Union.*

Mountain Messenger, Downieville — See *Gibsonville Herald*, *Gibsonville Trumpet*, *La Porte California Messenger.*

Mountain Messenger, Gibsonville.

Mountain News, San Andreas.

Mountain Whig, Sonora.

Muggins Mirror, Nevada City—Also known as *Miner's Spectacles.*

National, Quincy.

Nevada Democrat, Nevada City—See *Young America.*

Nevada Daily Gazette, Nevada City—See *Grass Valley National Weekly*, *Daily National Gazette.*

Nevada City Daily Transcript, Nevada City.

Nevada City Herald, Nevada City.

Nevada Journal, Nevada City.

Nevada Mining Journal, Grass Valley—See *Nevada City Daily Transcript.*

Nevada National, Grass Valley; *Grass Valley Telegraph, Grass Valley National Weekly.*

News, Murphys.

North Californian, Oroville—Became *Morning Advertiser.*

North San Juan Star, North San Juan — Became *Hydraulic Press.*

North San Juan Times, North San Juan.

Northern Argus, Horsetown.

Northern Journal, Yreka—See Yreka *Weekly Journal.*

Old Mountaineer, Quincy—See *Plumas Argus.*

Old Oaken Bucket, Downieville.

Oroville Mercury, Oroville—Later *Daily Mercury.*

Oroville Weekly Union, Oroville — See *Butte Record, Record Union, Chico Record.*

Oroville Register, Oroville—See *Butte County Register.*

Owl, Jackson.

Panamint News, Panamint.

Patriot, Iowa Hill—See *Dutch Flat Enquirer.*

Pioneer, Copper City.

Placer Argus, Auburn.

Placer Courier, Yankee Jim's, Forest Hill.

Placer Democratic Weekly, Auburn.

Placer Herald, Auburn.

Placer Press, Auburn—See *Auburn Whig.*

Placer Times, Dutch Flat.

Placerville American, Placerville.

Placerville Appeal, Placerville.

Placerville Courier, Placerville.

Placerville Herald, Placerville.

Placerville Mirror, Placerville.

Placerville News, Placerville.

Placerville Recorder, Placerville.

Placerville Republican, Placerville.

Placerville Semi-weekly Observer, Placerville.

Placerville Weekly News—Probably same as *Placerville News*, Placerville.

Plumas Argus, Quincy.

Plumas Democrat, Quincy.

Plumas National, Quincy.

Plumas Standard, Quincy.

Prospector, Jackson.

Prospector, Quincy.

Quampeag Coyote, Mokelumne Hill.

Quincy Union, Quincy.

St. Louis News—See *Gibsonville Herald.*

Standard, Quincy, Downieville.

San Andreas Independent, San Andreas—Became *Stockton Morning Independent.*

San Andreas Register, San Andreas.

San Juan Press, North San Juan—See *Iowa Hill News.*

Scott Valley Mirror, Fort Jones.

Scott Valley Semi-weekly News, Fort Jones.

Sentinel, Jackson.

Shasta Courier, Shasta.

Shasta Herald, Shasta.

Shasta Repubican, Shasta.

Shasta Vigilante, Shasta.

Sierra Advocate, Downieville.

Sierra Citizen—See *Mountain Echo*, Downieville.

Sierra County News, Downieville.

Sierra Democrat, Forest City—See *Georgetown Weekly News.*

Sierra Free Press, Forest City.

Silver Mountain Miner, Silver Mountain.

Siskiyou Chronicle, Yreka.

Siskiyou Herald, Yreka.

Sonora Herald, Sonora.

Sonora Mountain Whig, Sonora.

Sonora Union Democrat, Sonora — See *Downieville Standard.*

Standard, Downieville.

Standard News, Bodie.

Stanislaus Index, Knights Ferry—See *Knights Ferry Bee.*

Stars and Stripes, Auburn.

States Rights Journal, Auburn—See *Democratic Signal*, Auburn.

Student's Banner, Jackson.

Sun, Meadow Lake.

Sutter Creek Independent, Sutter Creek.

Times, Weaverville—See *Weaverville Journal*.

Trinity Gazette, Douglas City.

Trinity Journal, Weaverville.

Trinity Press, Weaverville.

Tri-Weekly Index, Placerville—See *Empire County Argus*, Coloma, *Argus*, Placerville.

Tri-Weekly Register, Placerville.

Trumpet, La Porte—See *La Porte Mountain Messenger*.

Tuolumne Courier, Columbia, Sonora.

Tuolumne News, Tuolumne.

Union, Yreka—See *Mountain Herald*.

Union Advocate, Auburn.

Union Democrat, Sonora.

Union Record, Jackson—See *Amador Dispatch*, Jackson.

War Club, North San Juan.

Weaverville Democrat, Weaverville.

Weekly Ledger, Volcano.

Weekly Democrat, Weaverville.

Weekly News, Georgetown.

Weekly Butte Record, Bidwell's Bar, Oroville.

Weekly Standard, Quincy.
Whig—See *Placer Press*, Auburn.
Young America—See *Nevada Democrat*, Nevada City.
Yreka Journal, *Semi-Weekly Journal*, Yreka.
Yreka Weekly Journal—See *Northern Journal*, Yreka.

The Editors

Alphabetical List of Mining Town Editors

Allen, James . . . . *Daily Transcript*, Nevada City
A'Neal, J. W. . . . . *Union*, *Chronicle*, Yreka
Anderson, James . . . . *Placer Herald*, Auburn
Anderson, W. F. . . . . . . *Nevada Democrat*, Nevada City
Armor, George . . . *Calaveras Independent*, San Andreas
Arthur, William . . . . *Union Democrat*, Sonora
Avaline, O. D. . *Sentinel*, *Central Californian*, Placerville
Avery, Benj. P. . . . . . . *Hydraulic Press*, North San Juan

Badlam, Alexander . . . . *Prospector*, Quincy
Baker, George H. . . . . *Granite Journal*, Granite City
Bail, Thomas . . . . *Plumas Standard*, Quincy
Barnes, W. W. . . . . *Herald*, Mammoth City
Bassett, James M. . . . . *Northern Journal*, Yreka
Beal, C. R. . . . . *Calaveras Citizen*, San Andreas
Bean, E. F. . . . . *Daily Gazette*, Nevada City
Beggs, William . . . . *Stars and Stripes*, Auburn
Bengay, J. M. . . . *Calaveras Chronicle*, Mokelumne Hill
Benham . . . . *Courier*, Copperopolis

Bennett, H. C. . . . . *Daily Union*, Grass Valley
Bireley, Rev. B. . . . . *Nevada Journal*, Nevada City
Boardman, J. H. . . . . *National*, Grass Valley
Bogart, R. D. . . . . *Lake Mining Review*, Mammoth City
Boggs, J. C. . . . . *Stars and Stripes*, Auburn
Boust, E. B. *Enquirer*, Dutch Flat
Placer Courier, Yankee Jim's
Iowa Hill Patriot, Iowa Hill
Bowman . . . . *Republican*, Placerville
Boynton, Charles . *Calaveras Chronicle*, Mokelumne Hill
Owl, Jackson
Sentinel, Jackson
Bradley, L. *Granite Journal*, Folsom
Briggs, R. M. . . . . . . *Amador Ledger & Record*, Jackson
Brown, H. H. . . . . *Union*, Yreka
Brown, N. P. . . . . *Daily Transcript*, Nevada City
Miner's Spectacles, Nevada City
Buckbee, John R. . . . . *Union*, Quincy
Bull, Oscar . . . . *Mountain Echo*, Downieville
Byrne, W. S. . . . . *National*, Grass Valley
Daily Union, Grass Valley

Campbell, W. . . . . *Sierra Democrat*, Forest City
Carter, W. L. . . . . *Pioneer*, Copper City
Casamayou, A. . . . . *Daily Transcript*, Nevada City
Caulkins, Silas . . . . *Fillmore Banner*, Quincy

Caystile, T. J. . . . . *Mountain Democrat*, Placerville
Cazneau, T. N. . . . . *Gazette*, Columbia
Chalfant, P. A. . . . . *Inyo Independent*, Independence
Chalfant, W. A. . . . . . . *Inyo Independent*, Independence
Charles, L. C. . . . . *Plumas National*, Quincy
Christman, Enos . . . . *Herald*, Sonora
Clark, M. B. *Prospector*, Jackson
Cole, Richard . . . . *True Republican*, Coloma
Central Californian, Placerville
El Dorado Union, Placerville
El Dorado Republican, Placerville
American, Placerville
Collier, W. J. . . . . *Bee*, Knights Ferry
Crawford, E. L. *Gem*, Georgetown
Crawford, J. . . . . *Democrat*, Weaverville
Crosette, George H. . *Weekly Butte Record*, Bidwell's Bar
Culver, E. S. . . . . *Scott Valley News*, Fort Jones
Curtz, Lewis . . . . *Plumas Standard*, Quincy

Daingerfield, E. A. *Ledger*, Volcano
Davidge, R. A. . *Democrat*, *Young America*, Nevada City
Davidson, Dr. D. M. . . . . *Scott Valley Mirror*, Fort Jones
Deal, Marcellus . . . . *Transcript*, Nevada City
DeCourcey, H. A. . . . . *Nevada Journal*, Nevada City
Calaveras Chronicle, Mokelumne Hill
DeGolia, D. *Republican*, Placerville

Delim, D. . . . . *Tri-Weekly Herald*, Nevada City
Dennis, J. H. . . . . *Independent*, Jackson
Dietz . . . . *American*, Placerville
Dinsmore, W. G. . . . . *Citizen*, Columbia
Donovan, C. . . . . *Union Democrat*, Sonora
Dormer, J. H. . . . . *Sierra Advocate*, Downieville
Dosh, Samuel H. *Courier*, Shasta
Duchow, J. C. *Gazette*, Columbia
Tuolumne Courier, Columbia
Duchow, W. A. . . . . *Tuolumne Courier*, Columbia
Dunn, J. W. . . . . *Mountain Whig*, Sonora

Eagon, J. A. . . . . *Amador Ledger & Record*, Jackson
Evans, B. H. . . . . *Scott Valley News*, Fort Jones
Ewer, Warren B. . . . . *Telegraph*, Grass Valley
National, Grass Valley
Ewing, W. . . . . *Folsom Dispatch*, Folsom

Fair, Capt. W. D. . . . . *Chronicle*, Yreka
Fairchild, O. L. C. . . . . *Observer*, Placerville
Fairchild, J. D. . . . . *Observer*, Placerville
Falconer, Col. Thomas . . . . *Gazette*, Columbia
Fellows, Hart . . . . *Stars and Stripes*, Auburn
Fitch, Thomas . . . . *Republican*, Placerville
Folger, Robert M. . . . . *Chronicle*, Markleeville
Forbes, W. J. . . . . *Sierra Democrat*, Downieville
Empire County Argus, Coloma

Foster, John S. . . . . *Miner's Spy Glass*, Nevada City
Francisco, Albert N. . . . . *Union Democrat*, Sonora
Freaner, George . . . . *Union*, Yreka
Fredonyer, Dr. A. . . . . *Old Mountaineer*, Quincy
Fuller, N. W. . . . . *Empire County Argus*, Coloma

Galloway, Judge R. . . . . *Sierra Citizen*, Downieville
Garfield, S. . *Miner's Advocate*, Diamond Springs, Coloma
Gear, H. L. . . . . *Plumas National*, Quincy
Gelwicks, D. W. *Miner's Advocate*, Dia. Springs, Coloma
Mountain Democrat, Placerville
Gilbert, Edward . . . . *Placer Times*, Dutch Flat
Giles, W. T. . . . . *Mountain Echo*, Downieville
Godfrey, G. K. *Vigilante*, Shasta
Goodale . . . . *Inyo Lancet*, Independence
Gore, George W. *Star*, Columbia
Gunn, Dr. Lewis C. . . . . *Herald*, Sonora

Hall, L. P. . . . . *Amador Dispatch*, Jackson
Placer Democratic Weekly, Auburn
Hamilton, H. . . . . *Calaveras Chronicle*, Mokelumne Hill
Harman, F. H. . . . . *El Dorado News*, Coloma
Harris, T. S. *News*, Panamint
Coso Mining News, Darwin
Hart, James L. . . . . *Northern Argus*, Horsetown

Hawkins, Hiram . . . . *Whig*, Auburn
Placer Press, Auburn
Union Advocate, Auburn

Heade . . . . *Gibsonville Herald*, Gibsonville

Heckendorn, J. . . *Big Tree Bulletin*, Calaveras Big Trees and Murphys
Columbia Clipper, Columbia

Helm, Alfred . . . . *Gibsonville Herald*, Gibsonville
Supplement, *St. Louis News*

Hill . . . . *Inyo Lancet*, Independence

Hinckley, J. C. *Republican*, Shasta

Hogan, E. T. . . . . *Plumas Democrat*, Quincy

Holmes, L. A. . . . . *Gazette*, Mariposa

Howe, H. J. . . . . *Democrat*, Weaverville

Hulbert, Horace . . . . *Gazette*, Georgetown

Hulbert, Maud . . . . *Gazette*, Georgetown

January, William . . . . . . *Mountain Democrat*, Placerville

Keene, James R. . . . . . *Shasta Herald*, *Republican*, Shasta

Kellogg, W. W. . . . . *Union*, Quincy

Kennedy, J. B. *Bee*, Knights Ferry

Kies, George O. . . . . *Mountain Democrat*, Placerville
True Republican, Coloma
Times, Coloma

King, Homer . . . . *Democratic Standard*, Jackson

Kooser, B. P. . . . . *Independent*, San Andreas

Lancey, P. M. . . . . *Gazette*, Columbia
Langton, J. C. . . . . *Mountain Echo*, Downieville
Laurence, J. H. . . . . *Free Press*, Mariposa
Star, Mariposa
Lewis, A. C. . . . . *Calaveras Union*, San Andreas
Lewis, John C. . . . . *Old Mountaineer*, Quincy
Plumas Argus, Quincy
Lewis, S. G. . . . . *Alpine Miner*, Monitor
Union, Oroville
Littlefield, Edward C. . . . . *Stars and Stripes*, Auburn
Lovejoy, John K. . . . . *Old Mountaineer*, Quincy
Lynch, Matt . . . . *Plumas Standard*, Quincy
Standard, Downieville
Lynch, Philip . . . . . *Placer Democratic Weekly*, Auburn

Marvin, John G. . . . . *Herald*, Sonora
Miller, W. H. . . . . *Daily Union*, Grass Valley
Mills, M. E. . . . . *Whig*, Auburn
Mitchell, Charles H. . . . . *Placer Herald*, Auburn
Daily Union, Grass Valley
Auburn Herald, Auburn
Mitchell, "Tabb" . . . . *Placer Herald*, Auburn
Moffitt, H. C. . . . . *Republican*, Shasta
Murray, Walter . . . . *Herald*, Sonora
McCallum, J. G. . . . . *Weekly News*, Georgetown
McDonald, Calvin . . . . *Mountain Echo*, Downieville
Sierra Citizen, Downieville

McElwain, Edward . . . . *Old Mountaineer*, Quincy
McNeil, H. B. . . . . *American Flag*, Sonora

Nixon, Robert . . . . *Journal*, Yreka

Oliver, J. W. . . . . *Columbia Gazette*, Columbia
Columbian Weekly, Columbia
Columbian, Columbia
Weekly News, Georgetown
Olmstead, J. P. . . . . *Star*, North San Juan
O'Meara, J. . . . . . *Calaveras Chronicle*, Mokelumne Hill
O'Sullivan, J. . . . . *Herald*, Sonora
Sierra Democrat, Forest City

Palache, J. . . . . *News*, Murphys
Parburt, G. R. . . . . *Columbia Gazette*, Columbia
Parker, James E. . . . . . *Inyo Independent*, Independence
"Parthenon" . . . . . *Quampeag Coyote*, Mokelumne Hill
Patterson, John . . . . . . *Miner's Spectacles*, Nevada City
Payne, George . . . . *Amador Dispatch*, Jackson
Penry, William . . . . *Amador Dispatch*, Jackson
"Peter Noodles" . . *Quampeag Coyote*, Mokelumne Hill
Poland, R. C. . . . . *Democratic Signal*, Auburn
Price, George F. . . . . *Union*, Yreka

Ransom . . . . *Courier*, Copperopolis
Reed, Myron Hill . . . . . . *Mountain Echo*, Angels Camp

Reynolds, Angevine . . . . *Mariposa Mail*, Mariposa
Ridge, John Rollin . . *Nevada Nat. Weekly*, Grass Valley
Roberts, George D. . . *Nevada Nat. Weekly*, Grass Valley
Robinson, R. E. . . . . . . *Tri-Weekly Herald*, Nevada City
Rockwell, E. A. *Herald*, Sonora
Rolfe, T. H. . . . . *Nevada Democrat*, Nevada City
Ross, J. W. . . . . *Star*, Mariposa

Sargent, A. A. . . . . *Nevada Journal*, Nevada City
Scobey, Joseph W. . . . . *Democratic Signal*, Auburn
Seabough, S. . . . . *Granite Journal*, Folsom
Searls, Niles . . . . *Nevada Democrat*, Nevada City
Selkirk, W. A. . . . . *Stars and Stripes*, Auburn
Shannon, John . . . . *Placer Democratic Weekly*, Auburn
Sharratts, George L. . . . . *American Eagle*, Sonora
Shepard, W. A. . . . . *Placer Herald*, Auburn
Sherman . . . . *Placer Democratic Weekly*, Auburn
Shipley, Henry J. . . . . . . *Nevada Democrat*, Nevada City
Telegraph, Grass Valley
National, Grass Valley
Shoemaker, Rufus . . . . . *Nevada National*, Grass Valley
Skelton, John P. . . . . *Nevada Journal*, Nevada City
Miner's Spectacles, Nevada City
Skillman, A. . . . . *Courier*, Shasta
"Slimface" . . . . . . *Quampeag Coyote*, Mokelumne Hill
Smith, C. F. *National*, Grass Valley

Sneden, Seth . . . . *American Flag*, Sonora
Snyder, Fred . *Miner's Advocate*, Diamond Spgs., Coloma
Empire County Argus, Diamond Springs
Spear, W. S. . . . . *Bugle*, Downieville
Spencer, J. D. . . . . *Mountain News*, San Andreas
Tuolumne News, Tuolumne
Springer, T. A. . . . . *Amador Ledger*, Jackson
El Dorado News, Placerville
El Dorado Republican, Placerville
Weekly Ledger, Volcano
Steele, R. J. . . . . *States Rights Journal*, Auburn
Stewart, Capt. W. Frank . *Empire County Argus*, Coloma
Stidger, O. P. . . . . *San Juan Press*, North San Juan
Nevada Daily Gazette, Nevada City
Marysville Journal, Marysville

Tallmadge, D. P. . . . . . . *Empire County Argus*, Coloma
Tallmadge, George E. . . *Old Oaken Bucket*, Downieville
Sierra Citizen, Downieville
Townsend, James W. E. . . . . *Union*, Grass Valley
Homer Mining Index, Lundy
Turner, J. D. . . . . *Union*, Yreka
Tyson, J. . . . . *Union*, Yreka

Urmy, J. B. . . . . *Tuolumne Courier*, Columbia

Wagner, A. . *California Staats Zeitung*, Mokelumne Hill

Waite, E. G. . . . . *Daily Transcript*, Nevada City
Nevada Journal, Nevada City

Walkup, Joseph . . . . *Placer Herald*, Auburn

Wallace, W. J. . . . . *Prospector*, Jackson

Ward, John S. . . . . *Plumas Democrat*, Quincy

Waters, Thomas . . . . *Star*, North San Juan

Weed, Ed. . . . . *Bulletin*, Greenville

Whicher, George . . . . . . *Stanislaus Index*, Knights Ferry

White, John . . . . *Herald*, Sonora

Wolcott, Oliver . . . . *American Flag*, Sonora

Yarnell, D. J. . . . . *News*, Placerville

Yarnell, H. A. . . . . *News*, Placerville

Youcham, D. . . . . *News*, Columbia
News, Murphys

Acknowledgments and Bibliography

I WISH to express my appreciation to the Librarians of various County Libraries of the sections covered, the Bancroft Library, and to the many friends who have contributed their knowledge to the compilation of this book.

The newspapers reproduced are from the collection in the library of The Society of California Pioneers.

Following are a few of the more important sources from which material was taken. To list all sources would make a volume in itself.

Annals of Trinity County, ISAAC COX, reprint, Eugene, Oregon, 1940.

History of California Newspapers, EDWARD C. KEMBLE, New York, 1925.

List of California Periodicals, issued previous to the completion of the Trans-Continental Telegraph, Aug. 15, 1846-Oct. 24, 1861. Thesis, CATHERINE CHANDLER, Stanford University, 1899-1900. California Library Assn. No. 7.

One Man's Gold, Letters and Journals of a Forty-Niner, ENOS CHRISTMAN, New York, 1930.

Pioneers, the engaging tale of three early California presses, CARL I. WHEAT, Los Angeles, 1934.

Records of a California Family, diaries and letters of DR. LEWIS C. GUNN, San Diego, 1928.

Saddle Bags In Siskiyou, ROY JONES, Yreka, 1953.

Shasta County History, ROSENA GILES, Biobooks, Oakland, 1949.

Southern California Newspapers, 1851-1876, MUIR DAWSON, Los Angeles, 1950.

Union List of American Newspapers, 1821-1936, New York, 1939.